# WITHOUT MAKEUP: LIV ULLMANN

# WITHOUT MAKEUP: LIV ULLMANN

## A PHOTO-BIOGRAPHY

compiled by
David E. Outerbridge

William Morrow and Company, Inc.
New York   1979

8-79   B+J   1500

**Library of Congress Cataloging in Publication Data**

Outerbridge, David.
Without makeup, Liv Ullmann.

1. Ullmann, Liv. 2. Actors—Norway—Biography.
I. Ullmann, Liv. II. Title.
PN2768.U409     791.43′028′0924 [B]     79-451
ISBN 0-688-03441-1

Printed in the United States of America.

First Edition
1 2 3 4 5 6 7 8 9 10

BOOK DESIGN: A GOOD THING, INC.

This book is dedicated to
Tom Abercrombie and Lloyd Dyer
of 700 Acre Island,
whose reign thereof, in a way, allowed it to happen.

In addition, I would like to acknowledge help.
For assistance in documenting productions:
Jon Stenklev and the Norsk Film Institute,
Annette Murer and the National Theater,
Eduard Baro and the Norwegian Theater,
and all the photographers, theaters, and film companies whose work is presented;
for the keenest of eyes: Ellis Amburn;
for expediting the entire process of compilation: Kathy Rosenfield and Marnie Hagmann;
for frightening production schedules: John Ball;
and for his knowledge of historical antecedents for the interview: Ivan Kats.
Finally, of course, without the cooperation of the Ullmann family it would have been a different book.

4

# Contents

# Introduction

We invest so much in our dreams and hopes.

Once we were children who woke up on the morning of our confirmation day. The day we had longed for through so many years, the day when a change was to take place, when adult life was to begin, and with it the right to make our own decisions.

And in a framed photograph we line up for posterity, next to other pictures in which we are infants, five-year-olds, school children, brides.

We stare out into space, never to exist again.

Soon I will be an old, white-haired lady, into whose lap someone places a baby, saying: "Smile, Grandma." I who myself so recently was photographed on my grandmother's lap. I who was picking flowers just the other day cannot fathom that it may all be over tomorrow.

                    Liv Ullmann, in *Changing*

So it is with photographs. They are bullets of time that punctuate a life, and are all we have as a reentry into the past.

This is a happy book. It details the life of an actress who in the breadth of twenty-two years of work went from a "Certificate of Merit in the Art of Speaking Verse" (with her name misspelled) to the position of the leading dramatic actress of our time—at least critically, if not by box-office measure.

Although the book was conceived as a biography in photographs of that career and, to the degree it is, a personal biography, I did not undertake its compilation for that reason. Almost every "celebrity" of the stage and screen, sooner or later, finds him or herself published in pictures. We, the fans of Humphrey Bogart,

Ingrid Bergman, *et alia,* can thus savor at our leisure remembered moments of the melodramas we wept at, the comedies we laughed with.

But Liv Ullmann does not quite fit that category. Most of what she has done on stage was never seen outside her native Norway. Her film career has also been uneven in terms of visibility and durability to audiences beyond Scandinavia. Except for the Bergman cycle of films and the lyric beauty of Vilhelm Moberg's *The Emigrants* she remains somewhat obscure. Even these films, moreover, while finding large audiences on the two coasts of the United States, never deeply penetrated the land in between.

Yet it is a strange and true fact that when Liv Ullmann is in America in performance she commands a space in the periodic press quite out of proportion to her general renown. And here is the question that this book explores: Why? Perhaps there are two answers. One of them can only be understood by seeing her in performance, for the words of a play or a film and the interpretation that are given them belong to the moment and the audience that shares it. The moment passes as quickly as the breath is spent.

The second answer has to do with the visage that conveys the emotions of the words. This book is about that visage and the persona underneath. It is a composite portrait of an actress who, extraordinarily, walks into each new performance in one essential way the same: the wigs, putty, dyes, and paint that are the makeup man's tools of disguise are not there. As a result, Juliet, Nora, Marianne, Saint Joan, and all the other characters of drama must be created from the same eyes, mouth, wrinkles, chin. Yet one can see her change, even within a single production, from innocent to sophisticate, youthful to mature, or old to young.

When one looks at the panoply of performances and across the decades of her life that they span, one is struck also by the dichotomy of sameness/difference. Her graduation portrait and a photo taken as her book was published in 1977 look as if they were taken with only a change of clothes, yet twenty-three years separate the two. On the other hand, her dramatic characters look like different people. The physiognomy of her face also plays another trick: it can move—without, I imagine, her being aware of it—from features of arresting beauty to ones of anonymous ordinariness.

Actresses do not exist beyond their time. A few, the celebrated, are recalled. Biographies of Fanny Kemble, Eleonora Duse, Ellen Terry persist, but are read only by lovers of theater. Have we lost something by ignoring this past? Probably not. Essentially, the art existed within the medium, cannot be re-created. Different, however, is our opportunity: through the marvel of photography we are bestowed with a panoply of exposed nerves and feelings by which we can know better the antecedents of the actress we are seeing in performance now. I also think that to see Liv Ullmann

ten years from now as Medea, Saint Joan, Judith Hearne, or some as yet uncreated character will be to appreciate and understand that performance better.

It is my belief that any person's work stands as a signature on the time given. It really does not matter whether others say that the signature was brilliant, clumsy, electrifying, or forgettable. It is indelible and belongs to the signer. Earlier this year Shoji Hamada, the greatest potter of our age, died. Unlike most contemporary craftsmen, he never signed his work. "The pot," he said, "is my signature." So, to me, this is a book of Anne, Nora, Joan, Marianne, Anna, Eva, Kristina, a woman . . .

Some of the productions are represented by one photograph, others by many. Often this has been dictated by availability and/or the quality of what was taken. Pictures from private life are generally bordered with a line unless they are full-page; off-camera and backstage photos usually are not unless it is necessary to isolate them from the actual production stills. I have attempted to provide textual material that brings the productions to life. In addition to my own comments I have included reminiscences and observations from Liv Ullmann. Some are drawn from *Changing* but most are from my interviews with her.

# On Acting:
# An Interview with Liv Ullmann

"On Acting" is a composite of several interviews conducted during the run of *Anna Christie*, which opened in Toronto in January 1976 and then ran on Broadway through June of that year. The interview might also be entitled "Without Makeup," as it penetrates the actress's very being. We are offered the secrets of her art: how she is able to distill the essence of each new character. This, in turn, leads ultimately to a revelation of the sincerity of an interpretation.

In this production of *Anna Christie*, Ullmann is Anna, John Lithgow is her lover, Mat Burke; Robert Donley her father; Mary McCarty his woman. It was directed by José Quintero.

—David E. Outerbridge

## January

David:   I would like to start by reading two opinions of the extent to which an actor should use his emotions within a character's. Diderot wrote: "Actors impress the public not by when they are furious, but when they play fury well. The tribunals, assemblies, everywhere where a man wishes to make himself master of others' minds, he feigns, now anger, now fear, now pity, now love to bring others into these diverse states of feeling. What passion itself fails to do, passion well imitated accomplishes."

The actor Tommaso Salvini said differently: "If you do not weep in the agony of grief, if you do not blush with shame, if you do not glow with love, if you do not tremble with terror, if your eyes do not become bloodshot with rage, if, in short, you yourself do not intimately experience whatever befits in the diverse characters and passions you represent, you can never thoroughly transfer into the hearts of your audience the sentiments of the situation."

Liv:   It is not a contradiction. They are both actually saying the same thing, though the first is more articulate. But Salvini is right too. What he doesn't say,

however, and what is the truth, is that it should not be *his* anger, it should not be *his* blushing. It should be that the character he is playing is so free inside of him that this character has the possibility to use his—the actor's—blushing, to use his anger. If you come onstage with a private anger and you think: "Now I'm going to use it," because you are angry anyway; or with a private grief: "I'm so full of sorrow I'll really be able to cry onstage," and you do it, it will touch nobody because it is not the character's tears, it is *your* tears. One is saying that you must imitate it, you must show anger. The other is actually saying the same: you must show anger but you must use yourself, use everything you know about anger.

D:   There is a whole school, of course, that believes that if I'm going to cry about a dead child, I have to think of my own dead child.

L:   That is partly Stanislavsky's Method. To me it is wrong, because you can do that a week and then you have used all the expressions of your feelings. Also I don't like the thought of actually *using* your dead child. Sometimes when I'm very tired I will know in a particular scene I am supposed to cry and because I'm so emotionally low anyway I can use that, and if I get some tears coming out at least the audience will see that the character has an emotion.

If I have something sad I can use it for about two or three days but then I can't use it anymore because it is used. I have to find something new. That is a kind of Method acting. It really doesn't work in a long run. You must find a technique that enables you every night to show or imitate anger by knowing so much of the past experience of your own anger that you know how it visualizes, and by visualizing you actually feel it. It is using your own anger, it is like your anger, but it is in the character.

D:   Maybe anger is a poor example. Anger is easier to show.

L:   Oh, anger is one of the most difficult. You can

always be pitiful, there are many ways to evoke it. Cry? The audience will think that you are crying just by placing your hands over your eyes. They will recognize that as a sign of crying because they are used to that sign. But anger—if that isn't real, people will know it immediately because it is such a broad display of feelings.

D: But isn't "broader" easier?

L: No. It is more difficult. Bigger emotion is much more difficult, both in comedy and in tragedy, because if the bigness is not filled, it looks phony. But it gives you much greater credit if you are able to fill it, are able to do it well. Then you do a fantastic scene. Take the scene in *Face to Face*, where Jenny has a breakdown and goes into a fit of alternating laughing and crying. That is a big scene, and I did it well. But if I had done it badly it would have been the most awful scene in the film because it would have been so obvious. So the bigger it is, the more true it must be for the people not to recognize it as falseness. The scene I look forward to on evenings when I know I'm with it is the big scene in the third act of *Anna Christie,* when Anna has her big outburst against men and their double standards. A whole range of emotions from love to rage, hysteria, and finally despair and hopelessness. But it is a long dangerous scene, too, because if I am tired or even if I'm emotional, I use private emotions. Sometimes I think I am good but I am not: I think my private emotion is enough. Or I overact because I am tired and I feel I have to do a lot of things to get the emotions across. No, the big emotions are much more challenging. In the quiet emotions you are always, in a way, safe as long as you can keep the concentration.

D: You say the big things are more difficult because they're big, but there is less subtlety, isn't there, which makes them easier?

L: They are "easier," if you say that "easy" is the same as looking great.

D: In big emotions like anger, does it take the same subtlety? Are the little details of the technique as important in the big emotions?

L: No. You can go more in a flow there.

D: So shouldn't it be easier?

L: No. Because how do you awaken a flow night after night? No, you must find images for that flow to keep it going and you must *not* overact just because you are not feeling anything and you think "I must give more now." You do not have the small subtleties that you have in a more quiet scene, and that's why it is very important in a big emotional scene to find a lot of "hangers": different images that you will recognize when you're there. Points where you have a certain movement, a visual memory, when you start to touch your dress—small things. A gesture of your hand will get you on in a strange way.

D: Do most people have what you call hangers?

L: I don't know.

D: What is a hanger?

L: Now I'm here touching this chair and on this I rest this line. That is to me a hanger. Method actors do not have that, I believe. They have to rely on floating on their feeling and knowledge of the dramatic background.

D: When you say hangers, do you mean reminders?

L: Reminders, yes, you can call it that. Emotional reminders provided by doing the same thing each evening. I know clearly what each little sequence should be about and so I can even miss one bit and still have a chance to recover because during rehearsal or from doing it so much I already have a bridge to the next sequence. If I slip in one segment of a speech, I can still save myself by knowing, from the hanger I am at, what I shall do in the next. If I was then only using my private anger, I would skip all the bridges and all the bits and be great in the first minutes and then suddenly maybe my anger would be over. And where would I be? But in this way I know I will look to the right for a while, for example, or touch something, and I have a lot of these technical hangers to take me through that scene. But that also requires that your co-workers be consistent. If they start to expand, making the scene into a different series of reactions, then you lose some of your hangers because you have to react to what happens.

D: Why?

L:   Because it is not a monologue. You are not alone, and some actors feel very in need of giving. They feel that the more they do the more they give other actors, which is true sometimes and not true sometimes, because each actor has to construct his own images and you might demand from him a very wrong image at the moment he has his own. I have a line, for example, where I have had a great outburst*; it is very quiet and I say, "You don't say nothing—either of you—but I know what you're thinking." If they are not two pieces of furniture there—really not saying anything—why do I say that? The father now starts when I turn to them— and I have a long pause just staring at these two men unable to give me anything—and then say my line, "You don't say nothing. . . ." Well, I have the father doing an enormous show of guilt and pity. He is saying a lot. So my line has to be spoken completely differently. With another actor, I might think, Okay, that guilt looks very real to me. Then my line, "You don't say nothing, either of you," would have a different meaning because it would also imply: "Okay, I see you're guilty but you're not saying anything," and I would say it in a different way; and my bridge to getting down to the chair would be different, because I wouldn't go down turning away from them, I would go down looking at him: "I know what you're thinking."

D:   Now, you could say that the father naturally would feel guilty when he suddenly hears this horrible thing.

L:   But there are moments for what you feel and there are moments for what you show, and O'Neill hasn't made a scene about the father feeling guilt. Actually the father leaves the scene disgusted with me, Anna, when it is over. That is what his scene is about. He comes back two days later with his guilt. If he already feels the guilt in the middle of my speech, what, then, is the scene about? Although how interesting to feel the guilt and not show it to the daughter—but pour it out in anger. That is to me interesting acting to show the opposite of what you feel—but in a way that the audience will recognize the feeling. Another actor might not make it a guilt thing, but he might make a big reaction here. I can't take away from another actor that if

*Anna, driven by the insensitivity of her father and her lover, has just told them of her life as a whore in the Midwest.

he wants to give a reaction, he has that right, but if it is wrong, it spoils the scene. This particular scene happens to be her confession, and because you are not alone on the stage what the others do has a lot to do with you and how you react.

I will make the point another way: when you're saying something very ordinary to somebody who is making a big reaction it is difficult to go on because you have to counterreact to his or her big emotion. In real life I can cite an example with my mother. I'm going to say a normal farewell to her, as I am leaving for the evening. We will see each other the next day. It is very hard for her just to say good night. My mother says something big and then my "Sleep well" has to become very exaggerated just to prove I have a true reaction to her reaction. If it is a play about that, then it is wonderful; two people making farewells into two different things and throwing away normal reactions. But there is also a place for a normal farewell and then it should be performed as such, without one of the two coming out looking shallow.

All actors have different techniques; some have their hangers, and some are purely emotional. I'm not entirely technical. But I am more technical than some actors: I'm more predictable. It comes out of a training of more than twenty years in repertory theater. I try to be pure in what I do. I use my emotions. I use them in the context of the character. I use everything I know about myself. In act two of Anna Christie, for example, in which the father tells me a hundred times about the "old devil sea" and our family, I am thinking that this girl since she was five was never loved, never wanted, and suddenly she is sitting close to her father. She has a father. I mean, she is almost back to being five years old, and it's foggy, and everything is wonderful. I never thought of this during rehearsals, but in the last weeks I have started to carefully, very carefully, put my hand on his knee. Maybe it is something she has wanted all her life, something I don't think the audience even will see. One person will see it and will understand. Here, the actor playing the father could have the right to stop that move. He could say: this scene is about me talking about the relatives and the sea. You are falling in love with the sea and I am trying to warn you against it; this is not about the little girl finding her father. He has not made that argument and I believe I can add my little touch on his knee to the scene. One can add anything. But, if this takes away from the other actor, from his speech, he has a right to say that it is an imposition on his interpretation of what is happening. But if not, then it is an addition.

D:   So even with hangers, which give you consistency, "predictability," you do change, don't you?

L:   Oh, yes. But I would rather call it adding to the character. When it is good, I would call it *adding,* at least. If you play the part long enough you will get either better or worse. You do change. You either enrich your part or the opposite. I don't change so much from night to night but I do find out a lot all the time about the character. It is inevitable when your instrument is your body, your voice and your emotions, your experience. I know much more, or feel much more, about the mature woman, the understanding woman in Anna now than, for example, when we opened in Toronto. I see her as a very liberated woman using all the freedom of knowing who she is, and having respect for herself, which I didn't in Toronto. I understand that this man Burke, her lover, is a child. I mean, the only way I can get down on my knees for him now is because *he* needs it.* Otherwise it is silly. I'm not doing it because I think we must have this pact. I'm doing it because I am free enough in myself to understand that it's impossible for him to take me if we don't go through this ritual.

D:   The getting down on the knees never really seemed right to me.

L:   It still is not quite right. I'll do it right one day so that you know why she does it. I know why I do it now: because if I was with somebody I loved and I knew they were in a lot of pain and they had to diminish themselves so much that they had to ask me to swear on my daughter's head that I wasn't unfaithful, even if I reacted against it, I would do it because they needed it. Without it they wouldn't be able to go on. So why not go down on your knees? If they need it.

D:   I understand the principle, but to me it's unnatural there.

*In the final act, Mat Burke asks Anna to swear on a cross on her knees that he is the only man she ever felt love for. Anna has already told him this several times previously, but for him to believe, he needs assurance.

L:   But I'm trying to go down on my knees so it's— I'll work on that. I want to go down on the knees . . . If it had been a film it would have worked the way I do it now: She stands a little because she doesn't know what he wants her to do and she is always, in a way, smiling, open for what he needs. And then she understands. He needs this to be a real vow. She knows he's religious. He's Catholic. She waits a little longer, then she kneels and stretches forth her hand because she thinks he's going to give her his cross. And she says, "Give it to me." I'm trying to say "Give it to me" in a way that he understands "Here I am."

D:   Coming back to the hangers—what happens to them that permits differences between two performances?

L:   Oh, you can leave your hangers suddenly. Because you have the security of the hangers. Then it is emotion, a kind of flow you can feel in your most real moments in life too, and if you suddenly feel it you understand something about the character because you suddenly understand something about yourself. Then you can leave *all* your hangers that evening because you have the confidence. You know, "Jesus, it's just there; forget the hangers. It is happening in this moment. Nothing can stop me in the scene now."

But it is not *my* emotion. It is just that I am so free that everything in me can now come out. It is using what I know about my emotions. It is my blush. It is my voice in anger. But it belongs to the character. Oh, then it is fun. It is theater enabling you for a short moment more life.

Anna is happy. You suddenly understand. Perhaps you even think of a time when you were that happy. But it is Anna's happiness and you feel it. You are a catalyst, and you feel this happiness. Then you can just let it go, flow from you, because it will come.

D:   But if that happens one night, if that marvelous thing happens, and you are happy because Anna is happy, would that happen the next day?

L:   Yes, because you would remember. One night I really felt strongly when the father said, "Can I kiss you?" I had already started to do the thing with my hand on his knee and I felt, "This is her first real kiss." Nobody sees it, it is not a big thing, but I feel that it's very important to show this element of Anna's longing for her father. And the "Can I kiss you?" opened something in me. It was Anna, but Liv understanding what Anna must have felt then. The cry my mouth made, it was a kind of crying, I knew what my mouth did, and tears came to my eyes but they were hers. And I know it was quite beautiful. I have been able to sustain that kind of smile-cry every night. I don't *feel* it anymore. Because it wasn't mine, it was hers. But if it had been me that was suddenly touched by the situation, I could not do it the next day. But still it is *me* having that kind of smile-cry.

That is why I disagree with the argument that you can use your dead husband to mourn the dead husband on stage. How long could you do it? You can't keep that. In real life, even, grief gets less and less. Just think if you use it on a stage, how it becomes. Part of the Method is locating a happiness or sorrow from your past that was significant, and using it. Emotional memory. But if you do that the memory will lose its flavor. Therefore it will become useless as a tool. Worse than that, I think it is an immoral use of our private lives. I remember the sorrow of my grandmother's death—I wrote about it in my book—but if I used that on stage to get a character into sorrow I would have sold out a private feeling and sold out my grandmother.

D:    Tell me what is happening when you wrote about rehearsing a scene for *Face to Face* where you are going to break down. Your daughter Linn comes in with milk on her mouth while you are trying to memorize lines. You wrote that "in a few days when I speak these lines before the camera I will have tears in my eyes because I will suddenly remember Linn the way she is now: . . . unaware that I hear almost nothing of what she is saying." What's happening there?

L:    Well, we are there talking about *films* where you can use these tricks because it is a onetime experience. Not like every day on the stage. Also what I think I meant about Linn coming in with milk around her lips was that I did not at the moment observe it as an experience that was going to change my life a little by feeling an emotion. But three days later, it would really go through me, the milk mustache. Something in me will suffer, and if at that moment I'm in front of the camera, that experience will make it easier to cry.

D:    Getting back to the point of developing the character during a run, don't you sort most of this out during rehearsals?

L:    Some of it, of course. But, you know, until the last few years or so I never asserted what I thought during rehearsal. I know the more I work the braver I will be about saying if it doesn't feel right, if the blocking isn't good for me, and not always feeling that the director must know better. Though I do know that if blocking feels bad, it may be good, but if it does not work for the actor, it is not good anyway. There must be another solution. Today, I know things that I can do, I know things I cannot do. For example, I prefer to stay in one place and move around as little as possible, unless I have a real reason. I am impossible taking a thought-walk across the stage, and not knowing why I do something makes me always act badly. If I can sit or stand or make a deliberate movement I am much better. I think part of the creative work, the older I get, will be much more realized in rehearsal because I will become more able to speak my own will, to express what feels right for me, not just accept the blocking from somebody else. I also feel much freer today to rely on my own feelings and my own experience, my own understandings, and not be ashamed to explain these to the director.

D:    But why don't these intuitions come out when you're trying to find your way into the part?

L:    Because there are so many things in rehearsals, so many things that are difficult to overcome. You don't always know during rehearsals what the difficulties are that you should overcome, and what are the ones you will *never* overcome and that would be much better to change, by finding other solutions. And the kneeling we were discussing—actually I accepted it early because during rehearsal I never had this liberated feeling about Anna, that *he* was the boy and *she* was the free one. So she kneeled out of love and would have scrubbed floors out of love. Whatever he wanted. She kneeled as a kiss. I thought that was rather beautiful, then, to kneel together. But today I don't think of it that way.

Yes. I have changed in the part. A lot. And that also makes many things that were right before not right anymore. And José has been fantastic. He has allowed me. When Mat first enters he used to fall over me five times, grabbing. After a few weeks, I said that doesn't work. He should do it only once. Anna is used to dealing with men—she knows how to get away from that. So now he does it once, and she puts him off from trying again. Before, also, in the second act, I paced back and forth all the time, talking about the fog. Now, José lets me just sit there and just be happy about the fog as if I were at the circus watching a wonderful act. That is one of many reasons he is such a good director. He allows all that to change. To make it right for me. For Anna.

D: I want to question this thing of whose emotions are being used in another way. It appears to me that even though it's not *your* emotion, for some reason the last performances of a run on the whole are marvelous performances, and they *are* emotional.

L: Yes, but then you're saying goodbye.

D: But that would, it seems to me, contradict the question of the emotions coming in.

L: Well, saying goodbye to a part is emotional. You have been so completely tuned into this character whom you are never going to see again. So, it's not Liv. It is Nora for the last time. And whatever Nora ever meant to me. Now I have to leave her. It is not me with a tear over the farewell, although that will be there in the end also. But it is really letting Nora have everything that I have, because it's the last time. That's emotional, although it is not letting Liv have everything of Nora but letting Nora having everything that Liv has to give her.

D: And you cannot do that in *every* performance?

L: That's what you try for, but you are no machine. There are performances that are much better than others. But that has to do with many things, with yourself, with the other actors, and very much with the audience. At the performance you saw on Saturday, I was truly in a very emotional, low state. And I did what I said I should not do: I was trying to use that. I thought I would use my private despair on the stage. And it did not really work. That is one of the reasons I wanted to know from you what it looked like, because I was not in control of what I did. And I wanted to learn something from the experience.

D: But if, as you say, you are a technician, and following the argument, you know how to fake emotion, anger, or whatever it is, convincingly, it should not matter how you feel.

L: Nobody can all the time. Nobody. It's impossible. Look at the greatest actor we have, Laurence Olivier. You think he is the same at every performance? No way. Because your body and your feelings and your mouth and eyes and arms are just an instrument. You have to have many more than the four strings of a violin in order each night, and there is no way that all fifteen —or whatever the number is—are functioning perfectly. You can be the greatest technician in the world and that little sparkle, at least, won't be there. Because with all creative art, and I think acting is also creative art, that little extra is the little extra you bring onto the stage that day which will be different the next day, and the next. That is the little extra you bring to playing music, etc. What is *only* technique will never go anywhere, as one who is *only* a Method actor with no technical knowledge cannot.

D: Could you act a part that you had no relationship with in real life?

L: Sure. Because, what do I know, maybe I have. I'm not saying I am doing the whore in *Anna Christie* perfectly in the first act, but I know that if I had the possibilities to walk out in the world and study the whores and compare them with me and find our connection, I would sooner or later find the clue to the tired, drunk girl called Anna, who enters the bar coming from nowhere, going nowhere. She is inside me too, I must just recognize her by visualizing her. I think I could play everything. Because I think everything is inside me. All possibilities. I want to believe that. I have limited myself for many years as an actress, also in personal life, so that I have let just one part come out. What I call "openness," which is a sweet, nice part, and onstage when I was younger was "shining." But I am more than that and I have gone beyond that—I want to go even further. I think there is no limit to what you can do if you give all you have. Take the risks. Give your heart. And I am not going to let down my talent anymore. I think I have let it down and I have limited myself. On the other hand, I know there are many things I cannot do. I will never be good at doing plays in verse, the elegance of

Shakespeare. I have done a lot of Shakespeare. Or Greek drama or verses. Or women that are symbols. It is what I have done most. I think I can do other things better.

D: Because you feel them more or because of technique?

L: Because I think I have more technical knowledge than I had before, and because all the things that I didn't think were me are just pressing to come out now. I haven't given myself my due. No. In glimpses only. Coming back to what you said, are there things I couldn't do. Yes, there are things that I couldn't do in private and there are things I couldn't do onstage. Greek drama I say I cannot do . . . but I *would* love to do Medea. Maybe I could do that . . . but I do feel a limitation in verse . . . but maybe not. However, in verse there is already a kind of constriction. You know the freedom of your shepherd,* it's awful, slitting the throats of his animals. But the freedom of that is also something; and that is what I would like on the stage. Even killing a dream about myself that limited my freedom onstage. I want the freedom more than the dream, the beauty. Which I've never felt before. I would never dare, before, to take room—space on the stage. And I start to do that.

D: But if it's right for the part, why haven't you?

L: I guess that's where I am confused. No, not confused, that is where I have been late, because the part has also been me and it has never been right for *me* to take too much room. I mean, I hate to take applause. These last weeks have been the first time in my life I have come onstage and not been embarrassed by applause. I asked José to see if we could not have the applause. I find it so hard. Also, I think it is stupid. Why should I stand and curtsey for you when you applaud me? We have had an interchange. But okay, today I feel there is a kind of freedom to come in, stand there for a while, go away, come back. I have *real* freedom sometimes when I put myself on a spot on the stage, because that is where I belong and I think that just at this mo-

*Earlier, I had described the generosity of a Greek shepherd I had been filming, who, to offer lunch, had slaughtered one of his goats that was passing by.

ment what I'm doing is something important and so I'm standing there and I do my thing. And it is wonderful.

D: So you are now free.

L: But you see, I had these limitations to overcome. I think it was important that I did *Anna Christie*, which isn't considered the best play. It certainly isn't the easiest to do. And Anna Christie is considered to be a woman you mustn't play today because she is so "kneeling." To overcome that and to find that you can sort of make a Nora out of her has been a fantastic experience. You *know* who Joan of Arc is. You can be splendid. As I say, you can do the big scenes wonderfully if you are good. But the fun of it is suddenly to overcome something that isn't obvious. And maybe it is no more than that.

D: That is a good point.

L: Which I wouldn't have said if I'd gotten terrible reviews.

D: But it is hard for me to believe having watched you on the stage and in films that you don't on the professional level forget whatever insecurity you may have in personal life, to say: "This is what it needs here."

L: Perhaps, partly in *A Doll's House*; in films, lately. But it is very recent.

D: Well, do it.

L: Slit some throats.

## February

L: Oh, you know, we have done a big change on the kneeling. I asked José, can I just for once try the scene without kneeling. And he was very unhappy because he had seen it as a wedding ceremony. And I said, I want to try, even if it is wrong I would like to know what feeling I get by not kneeling, because I feel there is something wrong with my kneeling. He said, "Okay." I said to John, "I'm not going to kneel today." And he got very upset because *he* loves to kneel. I said, "But then *you* kneel, or let's talk about it." And he said, "No, no, don't say more. Let's see what happens." I didn't go down on my knees when I said my line, "What do you want me to say?" And *he* did. *He's* Catholic. With him kneeling—we're already holding hands—I very obviously follow him and that's why I kneel.

D:  That's terrific if it works.

L:  Oh, it's much better.

D:  José likes it?

L:  Yes. He loved it. Because that makes it a wedding ceremony, which he wanted. She is kneeling because she thinks it is a wedding ceremony. She's not Catholic, but he is. So for him to make a vow is natural.

D:  I want to discuss a different point today. You wrote about being given the script for *Face to Face* and you said, "From now on the character is mine, and somehow I must turn Jenny into Liv." I always thought you would change Liv into Jenny.

L:  No. I mean what I say, and I know it is not usual. Some actors do turn themselves into the character. Some, the character into themselves. Among those who turn the character into themselves, there are two different kinds. One, like Cary Grant, a marvelous personality actor, turns the character into Cary Grant, but it's always like Cary Grant. I would count myself as part of the second kind: I feel I also turn the character into Liv. And I *look* like me, I'm sure, *but I'm trying to use anything in me that would be Jenny.* Do you understand what I mean? I'm not turning Jenny into Liv.

D:  But that's what you say you are doing.

L:  By using whatever is in Liv that is usable for Jenny. But first I have to know Jenny. So I get as much knowledge as I can about what kind of person Jenny is and study what I do know about her. There are a lot of things that Liv doesn't do in normal life that are inside me and that I can let Jenny do.

D:  You say, "I'm going to turn Jenny into Liv."

L:  Yes.

D:  Can't that be very dangerous because it could be Cary Grant turning *every* character into Cary Grant?

L:  Put Jenny *into* Liv. And *through* Liv make Jenny come out. That is what I mean. I put Jenny into Liv and use whatever is in Liv to make Jenny come out.

D:  Charlie Parker once told a saxophonist, "Don't play it, let it play you."

L:  That was what I said in my book, too: Let Nora play Nora. I let the instrument play me. It's actually the same as Charlie Parker.

D:  When you are allowing Nora to play Nora, how aware are you of the distinction between you and the character—are you always conscious of *you* in the context of the stage, lights, audience?

L:  Always when I'm best, I'm very aware of the reactions of the audience whether it is quiet or not. I'm very aware of handling it. Now comes a pause and I can keep that pause, and then I can go on. The moment when I am not aware really of what I am doing, that is the point when I am not good and it is very difficult to find the character again or to find yourself.

D:  So you're really being very analytical, because at the moment that you're doing Anna you are really at some distance from her and kind of moving her.

L:  But it's like a violinist, I would think, only the difference is that it is through my own body and through my own face. I allow it to happen, but I must allow it to happen. It does not happen without my being in charge. Although it *can*. But very seldom then are you good. You can fool an audience like that at times, but it is very risky. It is like a drunken actor who thinks he is fantastic. They lose the self-critique, and they are awful. They come off stage and say, "Wasn't I wonderful?" when they have just destroyed the play. They make pauses and they "feel" so much. They must think that this feeling goes by miracle to the audience, and all the audience sees is an empty, self-indulgent face. So you mustn't be drunk or drugged, and you mustn't be full of your own emotions. You must allow the character's emotions to go, and the best moments are when you are in charge.

D:  Do you feel that if you're standing back and relating to what's going on with the audience it is different on Wednesday matinees or Tuesday evenings? Do you find that you have to act differently for different audiences?

L:  No. Oh, no. I never feel I have to act differently. I have decided how I would like to do Anna, but I do know that audiences do get different performances from me. The way they behave and react will make me either lose confidence in what I am doing so that I become timid and don't dare to do things because I think I can hear them whispering how awful I am. Or they can be so responsive and aware, that I feel I dare to do anything that I believe about Anna. That is why sometimes it is dangerous to read critics. I remember reading one newspaper that said I was overacting in the first act. I was so conscious of this when I went on that it became a mixture of overacting and Liv feeling clumsy. I came before the part. I was so full of the negative thinking that I could not act.

D: I want to bring in Diderot again, who in his discussion of acting stated that actors, in real life, will be insensitive people. Because they play so many parts they have to, in a way, have nothing of themselves: "Great actors, and the great copyists of nature in whatever art, being gifted with a fine imagination, broad judgment, with exquisite tact, with a sure sense of taste, are the least sensitive of all creatures. They are too apt, for too many things, too busy observing, considering, reproducing, to have their innermost hearts affected with any liveliness."

L: Well, I would hate for him to be right. And you know my defense was, before you started to read it— there are actors who are insensitive, that's obvious— but my defense was, when you have an art, where you really have to be an observer and self-aware, how can you then be insensitive? But then he takes the argument out and says so just for those reasons.

I think there is a potential danger in real life that, at times, things don't reach you because your life is so full of observing, imitating, being part of other things.

That is what Ingmar has been occupied with in his films: it is eating people, cannibalism. Even when you feel sorry for them you do it as the artist. And I write in my book, I walk by my child who is crying and do a wonderful scene of a mother in the film. The danger lies there. It is one reason at times I feel very unsatisfied with acting. I think also that awareness of that is part of what I'm striving for as a human being.

We are talking about being sensitive, and you would think that people who are in the arts, so very aware and observing, should be more sensitive to other people.

What I really think Diderot is saying is that they are so sensitive in their art, in observing, it becomes impossible for them to deal with life with the same kind of sensitivity. It is not completely true, because I think that many artists do find this ability in themselves.

D: But there is the potential.

L: Sure. Go blind, past real suffering, and react to it onstage.

D: Do you believe theater is best when the audience is deceived into believing it really *is* Anna Christie up there?

L: That is not what theater is about: that people should think we are who we are portraying. You are not coming into a magic place where we are trying to do a trick and you are convinced it worked because you really saw Anna Christie.

D: What are we coming to?

L: You're coming to share experiences, to identify. You're coming to see an actor you know, or a play you might love, you're hearing a writer's words about life that sometimes may ring a bell inside you. For the moment you are sitting with people in a dark audience and being a part of the shared experience. People take pleasure in seeing things they know about. Part of their happiness is what they recognize in themselves. Part of their happiness is recognizing somebody they feel they know in me as a woman. Part of it, therefore, we do together. It is not that you are to believe that this really happens right here and now.

D: I disagree. I think it *has* to be *Anna* we see, which is why it is usually better to see a play than to read it. At the moment it is realistic. Even if it isn't natural.

L: It should look realistic, and the more realistic the better.

D: But it's not natural. Nobody dies the way they die on a stage.

L: Did you see *Streamers*? It is the first theater performance I ever had to leave, because one man in the last act was killed—I know a lot about theater, I've been in it for more than twenty years—and, to me, he was killed. I suddenly understood that in a little while another one was going to be killed and I just could not sit and watch it. It became too real. It was wonderfully staged, acted. But in a way, I almost objected to it because it did not give me a chance, because they had created a reality to confuse you between stage and life. I think theater is theater and you should really know it is theater and enjoy that feeling. You should not be tricked into feeling this is happening now. Though at moments, of course, absolutely. You know, I don't really know my true feelings about this. I *do* want the audience to believe the woman I play—to share with her—her life on the stage.

D: But the audience doesn't go as a critic to see how it was different: is she going to be melancholy? etc. It goes to see—

L: To have an emotional experience. To be open and get something when you are open. Give something back by listening.

D: But that happens when the audience has become so moved that the relationship is there, the actor has become Hamlet.

L: Are you sure that you are moved by the person becoming Hamlet?

D: How else do you identify with his dilemma?

L: That is something else. Then you identify with a character that is written and it is so well done at the moment that you identify with the situation. But is not necessarily because the actor has become that person. It is because that actor has been able to *live that person in front of you.* You don't have to be suddenly shocked to realize, Oh, my God, it was Alec Guinness, and you were deceived. It shouldn't be like that. Part of the enjoyment is that you're watching Alec Guinness, really being so good.

D: Then you're coming as a critic.

L: No.

D: Sure.

L: Also that is part of the enjoyment. When you see a good magician, if he's good, you feel simpatico. Because he can suddenly turn to you and smile, then he does another trick and you are into it and he smiles again. If you go to a psychoanalyst, you know that person isn't a dearest friend. You even know you have to pay the person when you leave. So you're not deceived into thinking something but at the same time you feel you are completely open to give and receive information from that person. You are very aware that you are paying.

D: Take a group of little kids. And one of them puts on a grotesque mask, comes charging into the room and all the other ones flee. Now those kids at that moment must know that it is little Billy, but their terror is genuine. And so then, it is not little Billy who they're afraid of, it's the image.

L: Sure. That's what I have been saying. You are agreeing with my argument. It is what they *want.* The enjoyment of being scared. They allow themselves to not see little Billy's feet under the mask. You allow yourself to not see Alec Guinness's feet under whoever he is. Because you want the identification.

D: And if the acting is good, the identification will be complete.

L: Yeah, but then you are not deceived, you feel wonderful.

D: The actor may know very well what is happening, but the person in the audience for two hours is really thinking he is watching Hamlet.

L: I don't believe that. I believe that the best responses I can get are when the audience is a part of me, and part of my knowledge and experience, and part of its knowledge and experience. Part of its identifying with my Marianne in *Scenes from a Marriage,* for example, turns out to be part of them believing they're identifying with me. Me as a woman, not as an actress. Me, a woman through whom Marianne is visible.

D: Now, you're into the movies, which is a little different.

L: Or the theater then—*A Doll's House.* Even *Anna Christie.* They like the shared feeling of the character and the person playing it.

D: You think that's generally true? You're not making an argument about somebody who is professionally aware of theater?

L: No. There are *unhappy* things—like the two fat ladies who wrote me after seeing *A Doll's House*: How can you be so happy? They did not identify with Nora at all. They were thinking *I* was the one up there on the stage. They were never deceived thinking it was Nora. What made them unhappy was they thought that Nora was *me* and I was thin and beautiful and acting. That's deceiving.

D: What did they write?

L: They said, "We are two fat ladies and we're so lonely and life is so miserable, and we watched you in *A Doll's House*. It made us even more sad. How can you be so thin and so happy and so beautiful?"

That was one of my reasons for wanting to write my book. Because *that* is deceiving. When people—that's what I hate in acting: actors who do that deliberately. They're always wonderful, beautiful, gorgeous. Because where *people are deceived,* it's the opposite to what we have been talking about. People are deceived into believing that Charles Bronson is on top of the world because he turns every part into Charles Bronson. They never identify with a human being, they identify with this bigger-than-life Bronson. That's where all the sex symbols are dangerous. Because the audience doesn't identify with the part, but with a kind of on-the-surface perfect kind of person, Farrah Fawcett-Majors, or whoever. That's deceit. The other way round is not deceiving because—

D: Maybe deceit is the wrong word. I don't mean it in a negative sense. If the actor is so transformed that the character becomes a reality, that is a deception. It lasts for as long as the play, and afterward in the street the theatergoer may even not recognize the actor.

L: Yes, well, it is true that people when they meet me after a performance are always surprised I am so tall. But I think this is an interesting question you bring up, because I think people enjoy knowing who is doing what, but knowing at the same time this is a character in a play, a human being in a play—and I failed those two fat ladies if they think it is Liv Ullmann up there. They would have a greater experience if they could see it is Liv Ullmann telling a story about a woman who is happy on the surface. Because then they would listen and learn that this woman is not happy at all.

## March

D: When I was in Toronto you said that the audience was laughing in the wrong places because some of the lines sound dated; therefore, you changed the way of acting so that they were no longer laughing. And then you decided that was not being quite true to O'Neill and you changed back again. The question is, What are you doing? You can't change the words because they are O'Neill's, but where is it you can have that power?

L: Sometimes you can play against the words. And who knows, maybe that is what O'Neill meant. Mat Burke has some macho lines that got bad laughs. We changed things. Okay, he has to say it, but if he shows at the same time it is a little boy growing up, it is not necessarily laughable. The audience will understand and accept it. But if he plays it as if he were a big, strong man and if Anna believes that he is now going to "change" her, then it is laughable. And the audience should laugh, too, because she is obviously a mature woman and free to make her own choices. But if you see her understanding and accepting those words as part of him that is vulnerable you can work against the laughter, against what is there in the sentence. I can answer his bragging with a smile and then we don't get laughs. For a while we were very bothered by the laughs. And they were understandable because we did not do it right. We tried to take out some lines, and we did everything to not get laughs instead of working harder on discovering what is this really saying, what can we do here. Not to avoid laughs, because if they are coming they will come. Now *we* have a reason for doing it, we know why this is not laughable. But you must not work for those people who are laughing. *You must work for what you believe is true, and what other people in the audience will recognize. When we were in Toronto, we were catering to that part of the audience we heard instead of playing to the listeners.*

Avoiding laughs is just as bad, hurtful to the play, as sometimes trying to get laughs. I know that very well, because I seldom have funny lines to say in a play. So I enjoy getting laughs in this play because there is a lot of comedy in the part. I have seen how you can kill the laugh you are used to by really going for it. You understand? You *go* for the laugh and you lose it. I slowly start to exaggerate because I love that laugh and then suddenly I am anticipating the laugh and it won't come. So we have lost something. That is a great knowledge to get, you know: if you have a laugh and you're happy about it, not to start wanting it and expecting it, but dare to say it the same way *every* evening.

D:    Laughter must be one of the most fragile emotions to toy with.

L:    Yes. It is. It is a little tiny thing that triggers it. But don't go into that because I still don't know why they're laughing. I always get a laugh at one point in the second act. So I'm not trying to get that laugh. I just do it the same because I don't really know why they laugh.

D:    I know exactly.

L:    But don't tell me. Because I know what happened with "Gee, you hate yourself, don't you?" So many critics were talking about how well I say that line, and how good it was that I had turned a normal old-fashioned sentence into a kind of question so that people laughed. I have stopped getting laughs because I'm so aware of it.

D:    Can't you go back to one of your hangers?

L:    Yes, but my hangers are for the emotions and really not for the way I'm saying lines.

D:    Have you really lost the laugh?

L:    It is not a secure laugh. A chuckle. But I used to get a roar. John Lithgow has the same problem. "'Tis no lie I'm telling you about the women."* He used to get these enormous laughs because he said that so innocently. To be honest with you, I don't think he knew what fun it was, because I think John Lithgow himself said it. For him, it was like a true line. But of course, when they laughed he found out how funny it is. Now he makes a lot of it. It's not innocent anymore. It is just a chauvinist remark.

D:    But then it should be easy for him to go back.

L:    He is not innocent anymore. That is also what is

*A few moments earlier Mat has been speaking of himself in a swaggering tone. He says this line with earnestness.

very difficult: to keep your innocence on the stage when you have done it a lot.

D:    But there's no innocence at all, is there?

L:    Yes, when he said, "It's no lie"—

D:    He said it innocently, but there is no *real* innocence. Once you have analyzed the part and rehearsed it, and you have done it twenty-seven ways and then you have played it two hundred nights, there can't be innocence but there must be the technical ability to—

L:    To reproduce innocence. Yes, but one of the most difficult things to reproduce is innocence. Because innocence comes out of a spontaneity and you don't always know where and when you are innocent. John doesn't know, for example, where he is really innocent and where he is sweet. Then when he finds out and he thinks he is sweet, or tries to make it sweet, he isn't sweet anymore. The same with me: when I have heard enough times about a moment when I "glow" on the stage, when I come on the stage trying to glow, the glow is over.

D:    Do you think of the "glowing"?

L:    Oh, there are evenings when I think this is where I'm supposed to glow. I try so hard to glow. Ingmar has warned me. Sometimes I ask him what is the worst thing I do and he said, "Don't try to make your eyes sparkle. Don't sparkle."

If you come onstage and try to sparkle, you won't sparkle. The sparkle—or whatever it is—is unknown to you. It is the same with innocent things you do onstage. You become aware, and you lose them. That is why I don't want to know what brings the laugh. That is why laugh lines are so difficult: you must be completely uncommitted yourself, not wanting this laugh. Because, there again, then it becomes personal. You mix up the character with yourself. You want the laugh for your own ego.

D:    No.

L:    Well, of course. Why do you think I want to say the line funny? Because I just love them to laugh.

D:    It's a funny line.

L:    I know. But it is Liv that also wants to hear that

laughter because Liv takes great enjoyment of being able to make them laugh.

D: But your ratings have nothing to do with laughter. Bob Hope, if they don't laugh, big trouble. But for you—

L: For me it is the greatest achievement, because people never laughed before when I was onstage. Of course I want them to laugh. So when I forget about just using Anna Christie, but turn into Liv, being clever: "Look at me, all you who said I couldn't do comedy, look how well I can say a line," and when I say it the laughter doesn't come. The reason it was funny before was that I let Anna Christie say it.

D: But you are enough of a good technician today to be able to reproduce.

L: Laughter is too fragile.

D: Bob Hope does it, he can do the same joke a million times and always get a laugh.

L: That technique is much easier. You go onstage and say one line. I have a speech in private life in which I always make people laugh: when I tell about my Hollywood days, about me bankrupting all the studios. If I tell them about my miserable life, I make people laugh because I know the punch line. But you cannot do a play wanting to get your punch line. You must do the play, and if you stay with the play the punch line comes out well, and people will laugh. But if you concentrate on jumping from one punch line to another, you can't do it.

D: Well, I may be repeating, but you did say you have these hangers that stabilize the way you move, etc., each evening: controls for what you are going to deliver. But now you are saying that the laughs cannot be controlled in that way.

L: I cannot control what the people will react to. The moment I start to taper my hangers to their reactions, then they are not *my* hangers anymore. That's what I mean. They should be my hangers and I should be safe enough—

D: Don't you have hangers so you can *know* when you want understanding that she has innocence, or she has happiness, or she has some emotion.

L: Then I have hangers. But if I want you to laugh, what has that to do with Anna Christie? She would never stand there wanting an audience to laugh.

D: But Anna Christie wouldn't want the audience to be doing anything because Anna Christie is on a barge.

L: That's just it! Anna Christie is up there to be identified. But she is not aware of an audience, though maybe that would be good for her. That's the recognition everybody wants.

D: But then would she also want this funny line, "You really hate yourself."

L: No. She doesn't say that because she thinks it's funny.

D: She is being sarcastic and that is funny.

L: It's not Anna Christie wanting a laugh. It's Liv who wants the laugh.

D: It's O'Neill.

L: No, and that is why I cannot do it anymore because it really is not a funny line and I was surprised the first time they did laugh. But it was because I didn't understand that I said it funny.

D: You do say it funny.

L: And after this discussion I am afraid it is lost. Now I will lose the laughter forever and just think of this talk when I get there.

D: I understand you are saying that it is you, not Anna, that is looking for laughs. What I'm saying is, you, as a technician or an artist who can control the—

L: But that is emotional.

D: But laughter is an emotion. I am sorry to keep pushing this.

L: Yes, but that is from the audience, it is not *my* emotion. My hangers are not, "I will say this line like this, and this line like that." My hangers are, "I'm going through this emotion here and we'll have this kind of quietness there."

D: But you want us to feel sympathy, anger, whatever, on the part of the character. We can also feel laughter.

L: I cannot decide for you what you can feel. The moment I start to get a special kind of reaction on something like that I am in danger.

D: Before you ever get on the stage, you read the play, you decide how to interpret, how to play this woman. You figure out what you are going to do with this woman?

L: I want you to understand her.

D: That's right. And aren't you working at that point on what an audience should see?

L: Sure. But I want the audience to see this woman, recognize her. The moment I start looking for effect, to make them laugh over a funny line, then I stop wanting the audience to understand Anna. You understand?

D: I really do understand, and I'm playing around on what I think is an interesting point.

L: It is very interesting, especially what happens as we discuss these things that I am trying to do and some of the difficulties; then having you there observing in a subsequent performance what I had talked about theoretically. It makes me conscious in the way which is wrong. Almost *showing* you: look, this is what I meant. I put my hand on the father's knee, which so often gives me a wonderful feeling. And yesterday I was doing it to show you. That is something you should be aware of. It is like wanting laughs. We said that the actor is not to *feel* something. The ideal thing is that by doing the things that are right for the part, *that* gives me a feedback of feeling. When Anna puts her hand on her father, I suddenly get a feeling. It is not only allowing feelings to come out which belong to the character, it is also allowing the character's feelings to fill you. There is incredible enjoyment! Then you get a feedback of feelings that are really not your own.

D: Is that more likely to happen in a tender moment? When Anna is screaming at her father, you are really not angry at that point, are you?

L: I'm not angry. But it gives me a kind of release because I can use a lot of anger. I can use a lot of anger that I usually don't get out myself. Not by using my own anger, but by using the same sources of the anger. When my daughter is angry and goes into her bedroom

and slams the door, kicks down all the books, and screams, she gets release. It's very healthy. It is something of the same thing. Opening up those doors. But on those evenings I've been angry at the actor who is the father or at Mat for some reason and I think, Now I'll really use this anger on them when the angry lines come, it is never really good.

D: You say it is a nice feeling when you touch the father on the knee. Then the part has sort of a tenderness, father and daughter, and you *feel*. But you don't feel the anger? It is only a release?

L: I get the feedback there, too. I do the action and then the action feeds the feelings.

And now, you know, the father has started to put his hand on top of mine.

D: You're making love.

L: Yes, we're starting to make love and it is really lovely because I just know what she is feeling.

It is a wonderful experience to be that kind of catalyst. I believe that in many ways acting is very healthy if you can use it in the right way. Because you are very open to reactions and what they fill you with. You are very open, or you should be open, to what other people do to you onstage. To see what happens in you. Which is something not always open to a real world.

D: Are you saying while you are acting you become more sensitive as a person—the actor—or are you saying it makes you more sensitive in general? As a person?

L: I think I am very often more sensitive when I act than I am in real life. I think I am at the good moments of acting at my most sensitive, as I am only at my best moments in life.

D: Which goes back to the point that there is so much sensitivity being given in the part that in real life actors are, on the whole, rather callous.

L: Yes, we talked about that danger. But if you are very aware of what happens to you when these doors open, and you feel sensitivity, you can let that come to real life too. That is why I say acting can be a very healthy thing, used right. Because you learn to be sensitive. And it's something that you can adapt to real life.

I believe you can use acting in a positive way. It can enrich your relationship with people. There is also a great potential danger. That, in fact, you get into bits and pieces.

D: I remember a long time ago you said, and it must have been a criticism of acting, you don't like actors, you only like human beings.

L: Yes, because I think some actors are shallow.

D: Because they do so much on the stage?

L: No. I think that part of their shallowness is what allows them to be actors. I don't think that acting in itself makes people shallow if they were not shallow from the beginning. But there is a lot of pretense in this job and I think if you start off with a lot of possibility for pretense, acting will surely bring it out. But then I know a lot of actors that are real people. One also has to make a distinction between actors that work only in television or film and actors that work on the stage. Stage actors have to go through much more training, much longer, and in depth: practice, theory, thinking, and rehearsing. A film actor can turn out the memory of his dead mother and cry. It can be done because they don't have to repeat.

D: Diderot wrote: "I have often seen an actor laugh offstage; I do not remember *ever* seeing one weep."

L: That must be his lack of communication. Actors do cry. Jesus, I cried for two hours today.

D: His point is that actors do have children, parents, etc., and how can they possibly get out there and play night after night if they are so sensitive to all the demands of those other people?

L: Don't doctors operate even if they have families? Do they suddenly kill all their patients when they have tragedy at home?

D: Diderot: "Just as the doctor becomes hardened to blood, or the butcher to death, so the actor becomes hardened to emotions, because, having lived through so many emotions, he becomes less sensitive," the callus forms.

L: I don't think he is right. I think an actor is maybe better able to perceive when people act out false emotions privately. I think actors can see through them. Also, if they are sensitive and they have used their sensitivity to grow onstage, that same sensitivity will be there for an actor's private life as well. The vulnerability to what others are feeling or what you feel with others: if you have that for the stage, you have it for private life. I want to state my own case. My difficulty, really, is that I am "vulnerable," and that is my great strength onstage and I think it might be my weakness in private life—that I am very absorbed with what I think other people are feeling and thinking.

## April

D: I want to discuss close-ups in film. What are the difficulties? About *Scenes from a Marriage* you complained: "I knew that people would identify very closely with me, thinking this is my story. Then in the close-ups having to say things that were really the opposite of what I believed in was difficult." But if you're playing the part, why should you worry about that?

L: Because of what I have said before—the identification—and because the close-ups, as Ingmar used them, in the specific case of *Scenes from a Marriage*, are very close to the audience. He built the part so much on who *I* was, and because he was using that many close-ups I knew that other people would always think this is the story of Liv. And as an example, I don't want to deny God, the Faith. Making it ridiculous. In this movie, I had to do that in a big close-up. Because I was denying something then that is very important to me, I could only feel personally abused. I didn't feel part of those scenes. There *are* times when you are you.

D: Is there a difference in film? Suppose that that had been onstage, could you have done it?

L: I *did* it in the film because Ingmar Bergman felt it belonged to the part. I am talking about personal feelings. In a theater—where there is more space between you and the audience—people would not identify with me so closely, they would know this is a part, so it would not bother me that way. They don't think I am a whore just because I come in and say I am one. In a very tight close-up where you have to say something—I mean, there are so few things you really believe in. And it isn't fun to be in a close-up mocking what you believe in.

D:   Even though it was right for the character.

L:   I don't think it was right for the character.

D:   Oh.

L:   Maybe that's what it all comes down to.

D:   Did he give you an option? I know when Marianne talks about all her love affairs, you told Ingmar you didn't believe she would have had them.

L:   And then Ingmar allowed me to brag about it in such a way that you don't believe what I—my character, Marianne—is saying.

But you see, the denying God was a special scene. It was the setup; it was a filmed interview, where this woman I am playing is interviewed. And it was the first day of shooting. And there I was in a big close-up mocking God just because Ingmar wants to mock God.

D:   But it is not you, it's the character.

L:   I know it's not me. I know that. But I also know that many people believe it's me. And they will hear me say I think the Bible is ridiculous. I don't want to be the one who is going to say that to people. Because although I know that I am a character in a film, many in the audience take everything I say as me. Especially with Ingmar. There were so many critics saying this was *our* story, and he didn't make it less so by showing my childhood pictures. They even thought that was my diary that I was reading in the picture. That bothered me very much too, because it *wasn't* my diary.

D:   But you could play a part where you say the Bible is ridiculous, if it's right for the character.

L:   If it's right for the character. Because if the author has written his play to mock the Bible I would say, No, I don't want to be in that play. But if the author wants to do something whereby my mocking the Bible is making a point *for* it I wouldn't mind. Then I would be a tool in a play disgracing what the play wants to grace. This is what I mean: when I don't believe that this is what the character would say or do, then I hate close-ups. Close-

ups give you such an opportunity to be real. And how can you be real if you doubt what you are saying?

D:   Would you have trouble playing a part that you thought was immoral?

L:   Not if the play was moral. Not if the immorality of my part was the moral of the play. But, of course, you do always want to defend your character so you wind up finding the good sides.

If, for example, there is a scene telling a story about the confrontation between a mother and a daughter, and the point is that the daughter is the victim and the mother is the victimizer, you can play the victimizer any way you want to, simpatico, ruthless, whatever. But if the scene is about that, you have to play it. And if you are suddenly dealing with two victims, the interpretation is wrong. But then again, the older I get the more clearly I see that you can just as well deal with two victims—only maybe not at the same time—in the same scene.

D:   Perhaps "victims" are easier roles to assume than "victimizers."

L:   Well, you do look for the good sides. If I were Hedda Gabler I would try to make her vulnerable.

D:   Have you ever done *Hedda Gabler*?

L:   No, but I would like to because I have a feeling she's tremendously vulnerable and she hurts the people around her because *she* is so much hurting herself. It is the cry of someone really being caged in, and none of her acquaintances see it.

D:   Do you think you could act that with the same lines?

L:   I think it is all in the text. I would like to make Hedda Gabler—I mean, she kills herself, she is so desperate for attention. She burns manuscripts, she badmouths, she kills what she loves, she does everything.

D:   But what is it other than viciousness when she burns the manuscript?

L:   Well, that is such a big thing. Do you think she does that out of viciousness? I don't. I know once my mother kept a diary. It was at a time when I was angriest with her. I was fourteen years old and tore it to a thousand pieces. I am sure it meant everything to her. But I didn't do it out of viciousness. I did it out of anger because that diary was making me an outsider.

D:   Has Hedda ever been done that way, that you know of?

L:   It may have been.

D:   She is always a bad person.

L:   I don't think she is; maybe because I recognize so much of it in myself, though I am much more Nora's facade. You know, they are very much alike. Only Nora takes the sweet way out. And the other one takes the bad way out. But they are both protesting.

D:   It is always played the other way.

L:   Why? The reason is to find out why people are harmful. Oh, it's so wonderful: somebody sent me this from Rilke. "Perhaps everything terrible is, in its deepest being, something helpless that wants help from us." Isn't that beautiful? I mean, that is Hedda Gabler. It would be very interesting to show her that way.

D:   Do you think you could do that?

L:   How do you know Ibsen did not mean it? Everybody told me that Anna Christie was completely unliberated; how can you do such a play today when women want to come into their own? Well, the play is about a woman who comes into her own. It is in the text. I am not playing against the text. And I'm sure—it is a long time since I have read Hedda Gabler—but I cannot imagine Ibsen not using that possibility with his compassion for human beings—that he would just make an awful portrait of a woman.

D:   When you were doing A Doll's House in New York there was an interview with some specialist on the stage who was doing a book. At one point, he asked, couldn't you just say these five lines? It was from the last act, and you said, absolutely not. You said, I cannot do that. I can only do it onstage, acting is such a fragile thing.

L:   It is like asking a doctor at a cocktail party, can you look at my throat now? We are not puppets. There are actors who can do that but it is those actors you dread to be with who perform all the time and couldn't be more happy if you asked them to get up and do

something. To me acting belongs to the studio and the stage. In your private life it is an imposition to be asked to perform. I am even embarrassed about sometimes being with a group of people talking about some poem, and they ask, can't you read it since you are an actress? That poem, which was good for that moment, could be read by anyone as well as me. Actually, it would be worse for me to read it because then I would get ambitious and our reading the poem together wouldn't be the same. Because I would quit being only Liv, I would be ambitious that the poem be read well. Instead of shared.

My lines in Nora were important. They belonged to the whole content of Nora. Or that bit of Nora I had reason to show just then. But I have no reason to prove to someone that I can take any line and read it. Dick Cavett asked me: "You're an actress; say you love me in a way that I believe it." Gene Shalit asked me to act something so he would believe it was real in the interview. I think it's an imposition and I can't do it and I won't do it. I think that is prostitution. That is like giving your soul away for money when you used to give it away for love. It is the same. I could say "I love you" to Dick Cavett if I loved him but I don't want to sit there and be phony just to show I can convincingly say "I love you." Many people can actually do that. Especially in the United States, where you are "darling" with everyone. I don't think I could. If people tell me they love me, I believe them. It has nothing to do with acting. It has something to do with my needs: the value I put on words said in private. The difference I feel for the act and the private.

D:   But there are two different things. One is to say, on a TV show, because you are demonstrating acting, "Dick Cavett, I love you." That is fake. However, it is different from him saying, "Won't you please do the final soliloquy from A Doll's House?"

L:   No, it's the same. It would be faking. It would be like having to prove that I can convincingly say lines as an actress. That I'm not allowed in my private life to say things convincingly as Liv. This is what I mean: suddenly I have to say some lines as if I were an actress doing a part, and the way I act I must believe in what I'm saying there and then. Already then there is a contradiction. If I'm sitting and being truthful to this journalist in an interview and suddenly he asks me to switch and do an acting part, and since in acting I want to be truthful, too, I just can't. Then I'm faking.

D: It is different from the entertainer—say, a magician —who can do that.

L: Oh, I can do that, too. If I'm asked to come to a home to read poems, I can do that. That's why I am invited. But if a magician is suddenly asked to take a rabbit out of his hat, if he hasn't prepared, there's no rabbit there. He will only sit there with an empty hat and try to get something out of it. To satisfy the people.

D: I wonder if doctors do get asked to look at throats.

L: Listen, when this production was in Washington we were invited to one of the embassies. And Bibi Andersson, who was visiting me, wanted to bring two friends who were well-known entertainers. The hostess said yes, if she could ask them to entertain us during coffee. They said no, of course. It has to do with pride, too. But this thing with the interviewer has to do with shyness.

D: You said to him it was too fragile for experiments.

L: Yes, it is. I am shy because I can only do my work onstage. Privately I have less confidence in getting my lines right.

I have been asked in three interviews to say that first line of Anna's "Give me a whiskey. . . ." [Pause.] You see, even now with you I have dropped off the other line that goes with it because I can't say it. I feel phony.*

D: If it's technique, on the other hand, that allows you to rage or whatever, then why can't you do that here or there or anywhere?

L: Because there's no reason to do it. It would be just to prove something. Liv that has to prove something.

D: I want to pick up on something you said the other day. You said the performance was altered because you were aware that I was watching. How does it work, in general, when you have somebody close to what you are doing in the audience? Ellen Terry in her auto-

*The line is: "Gimme a whiskey—ginger ale on the side. And don't be stingy, baby."

biography recalls when she acted and Sarah Bernhardt was in the audience. She said that on that night she gave a fantastic performance because she was really acting for that person and she was doing things with nuances, that she was tuned especially well. That is one opinion. On the opposite side of it, when John Barrymore played Hamlet, the night he knew Stanislavsky was in the audience he so overacted that Stanislavsky literally could not face him afterward. How is it with you?

L: Closer to the latter, because all kinds of self-awareness, not character awareness—starting to observe oneself instead of the character—is very dangerous. We had Nureyev in the audience last week and immediately I started thinking, "Oh my God, oh my God, he's looking at my movements," because he is a dancer. My movements became more awkward because I became self-conscious. I know many actors do not want to know who is in the audience. Sometimes, for me it can be good if I am very tired and I have nothing to start with. No impulse: Oh shit, I don't want this anymore. Suddenly if you know that there's somebody out there really watching you it gives an extra—

D: If you knew Ingmar was coming tonight would you do better or worse?

L: I would probably do worse. Because I would try to do better and that is why I would do worse. For example, at the performance for the Actors' Benefit, there were only actors there. Everybody said it's a wonderful audience. It was not wonderful at all. It was a lot of actors trying to laugh and show they understand, very strained. And some of the points we were used to getting we didn't get at all. You want to show them, and you give a worse performance and they want to show they understand and demonstrate that. If Ingmar is there and something goes wrong, I will think, damn, this went wrong and it will take me half a minute to get over that bad feeling and go on again, and his face will come into my concentration. A known person sitting there will intrude into your concentration and then you are not in one flow with the part, you are in broken lines with the part. Or I will try with somebody like Ingmar to do something and the moment that I get into it I am wondering if Ingmar is thinking, she is doing "that" again. But if it is a wonderful audience and I feel they are with me, if it goes well, then it can be an extra thing that this person is there, because then I know it is going to be part of a lovely evening. I won't get in trouble and he will be with me. But the usual thing is that one does get thrown because people you know are out there.

D:   The hangers fail. You have learned your cues, so that even when you're happy or sad, you go on and Nora laughs or cries in the same way every night, yet—

L:   I'm not a machine, David, and I am afraid I should never have told you about the hangers. They are fantasy tools impossible to describe and when used against you, and not understood, become friends you gave away.

D:   No, you're not a machine. But you can put away a lot of your personal things. The fact that you had a terrible phone call, you can put away while you're being Nora.

L:   Yes, that I can put away.

D:   But you can't put away the fact that—

L:   —that this person is observing me.

I can put away something very upsetting that happened to me before I went to the theater and even use it. I will be so stirred up that the adrenaline is going, and you do function better when the adrenaline is going. You cannot use the phone call, but you can use the stirring.

D:   Do you find the performance settles down the longer the run?

L:   No. In long runs there is a tendency to become unbalanced. You start to do a lot of things and they become too big, and then they give another image than what you thought they did. Where you are now reading horror for the future, I think I'm showing pleasure and astonishment for the present. And that is the great danger. And that is where one always needs an observer like a director in the audience. It's very important for actors to have observers outside of themselves when the play goes for a long time. Because your internal observer starts to get tired. She thinks she does too little. And she wants to create more. Of course, it always ends up with being too much. What you had in the beginning was okay. The only new things must be

new subtleties. But never extensions of what you already did.

You told me after a performance last week you thought I made too much of the line: "I'd rather have one drop of ocean than all the farms in the world." I remember doing it big. I was really tired and I thought, Now I must pull myself together. And I really did it big to look good. And in my tired state of observing I thought I did it wonderfully. But most often it's safer to go under when you start to wear and tear than to go over.

D:   And what about the director? Doesn't he deal with these things?

L:   Oh, yes. José, when he came back from Washington, where we were touring, said this was a production gone sick. All productions do grow sick when they have been playing for awhile. And they go sick for small reasons sometimes. One person starts to speak a little louder than the others. Then the next person who has a tendency to speak louder gets louder and others follow, and in two weeks people are screaming but they don't know it, because it happens slowly. That is a sickness. Here, instead of louder voices we are getting into louder victims. The sick thing was not that we were playing it too rough, we were playing it too weak, too much for pity. So we all went for sympathy. One suffering more than the other.

You can play sympathetic. I'm not saying that. The play is—Hedda Gabler, she is the victimizer and the others are the victims. You can say that the victims also make the victimizer a victim. I say that is Hedda Gabler. But I cannot look away from her actions. I cannot burn the manuscripts like I was on a stake, Joan of Arc. What I have to try and show is, why does this woman do these awful things, say these awful things? If I want to defend her, what is it *in* her? Maybe she isn't an evil woman.

D:   Shaw wrote: "If you want to know the truth about Lady Macbeth's character, she hasn't got one. There never was such a person. She says things that will set people's imagination to work if she says them in the right way. That's all I know, I do it myself." Which is giving it all to the interpretation.

L:   Go home and read *Anna Christie*, O'Neill's line, "How are you any better than I am?" That's what Anna says to the man she loves. O'Neill maybe doesn't know the wonderful line he's giving her. He doesn't know the breaks he's giving for a human being. Of course, he knows it somewhere. But he's not necessarily aware of it. In a way it is his clean soul that has written that wonderful line. But it is as if O'Neill himself, the writer, doesn't know what a good line is. So he puts a parenthesis in front. He tells what the actress should look like while saying the line, and if she did his parenthesis directions, the wonderful meaning of the line would be lost. Maybe even the greatest don't trust their own power. I always cross out the parenthesis directions of a writer.

D:   But you, you say, I don't act against Ibsen. I can't change the words. You won't change the words, but you will go against the directions.

L:   Yes.

D:   In what way is that not violating it?

L:   It's not violating. It's trusting that his soul and his heart may have felt more than he was aware of than when he made these boring, dry stage directions.

D:   At what point does the interpretation come in for you? When you read the script are you trying to think, well, Ibsen must have meant this. When does this start? In rehearsal?

L:   First in rehearsal. When you read it for the first time there is the encounter: what kind of person is this? Very often that will be superficial, and if it is a very good writer, the more you work with it, the more you find. With Ibsen, you can do a play again and again with a year's interruption and you suddenly find oceans of new things to put into your interpretation. This is what differentiates the great playwrights from the small ones. The good ones just give limited possibilities. A great one, maybe two hundred years after it was written, is still modern, has to do with our time. And you can even put it in our day's costumes. And the way you do it is completely different than it was two hundred years ago and yet everything is there in the text.

Then, of course, there is the director, whose concept of the play is to be shared with the actors. José's concept of *Anna Christie* is, to put it in two words: destiny and the sea. His concept had nothing from the beginning, I

think, to do with a liberated woman. That came while we worked. That was sort of my feeling, but also destiny and very much the sea. Less the destiny. But for José destiny was a very important thing. So that is the concept we had, and that is what must be part of our interpretation. Because each actor cannot decide individually to play his character in such a way, without thinking of the whole concept. Because then we are doing monologues onstage and we don't have a play. The director must give a concept in which we all have to fit and in that fitting we give our individual interpretation.

D:   And that is left to you?

L:   That is under guidance of the director. If you are a strong actor, if you are a giving actor, and an actor with fantasy yourself, very much of it comes from you. Or, if the director knows you well, even if you do not know how to get it out, he will tempt it out of you. But there are also actors who have no feeling for a concept of a play and rely completely on the director. Or, worse, do their own play about themselves.

If the director's concept does not include part of your interpretation there must be a discussion and then either you or the director wins. If you are a good actor and he's a good director he will give allowances for your interpretation as long as it is true to the play as a whole. If José were a different director he might have denied me the liberated woman and I would be . . . a little lost. But we work almost like from heart to heart—that is our communication. So what is his becomes mine—and the other way around. He let me show Anna as a woman of today who grows into her own; maybe it was all his idea and he only led me to believe I gave birth to it: the liberation of Anna Christie.

## May

D:   Here's a comment that goes back to the question of personality—whose personality is it onstage? Michael Redgrave wrote: "The hardest thing is to be yourself on the stage. I remember many years ago Edith Evans saying to me, 'I envy some of you young people who start off your careers on the outset with a personality of your own. It took me years to find mine, peeling off layer after layer of myself like an onion. Until I found the essence.' I was mystified at the time for I knew that even from her first appearance she was said to have possessed remarkable authority but I know now exactly what she meant. What she meant was not of course the persona which the public and her friends knew, because all of us, whether we like it or not, have more than one of these. But the essence of her emotional experience and the residuum of a life's philosophy. This is the actor's face. The rest, her appearance, her voice, her technique, and her mannerisms, are the mask. But without the perfect discipline, the latter, the mask, the former will never be visible to us."

L: It sounds better than it is because, you know, if it is only the essence, that is denying that there is more than one kind of essence. There is one essence but there are many kinds of shades to that and peeling off means peeling off the shades.

You can never peel off what you are inside. I love the complications, the pain, struggle of unsolved things. Part of the persona will always be that. You can never become an essence. The technique to me is *not* having a mask. The technique to me is to make *it* invisible. I don't believe in masks. The more self-awareness I have and the deeper I have gone into myself, the more I have to give. With a naked face and body.

D: Are you saying that a good actress, and actor, really does it well if the personality of the actor and actress comes more out? or less out?

L: More out. But I am not talking about *the* personality; I am talking about all the conflicting, many facets, colors, pains, happiness that are within all the shades. Again, we must differ a little with actors. Let's say you are doing light, clever comedy. That is one special kind of technique and I think you can do that successfully and keep yourself comfortable behind a mask. You just have these wonderful *esprits*. But if we are talking about character actors, whether they are comedians or tragic characters, I do think the deeper the person has been going into himself and the more he shows of himself, the more able that person is to give a real performance. If you see somebody good on the stage, but it is something that just doesn't quite click, this person does not have the experience of his anger. He is

portraying it. It sounds good, he is not overacting, but it doesn't really go deep into the character and into the actor. It is sort of a portrayal.

D: I suppose if you asked ten people on the street who is the better actor, somebody whose character you can see, or somebody whose character—

L: They don't know. They might not know it also is a human being they are watching, that the actor is presenting something in himself. They identify with the part.

D: So the truism that the better the actor the less he is going to let his own thing in there and the more it is going to be a mask—

L: On the contrary.

Let's say it's me. And someone watches Anna Christie. They would think it was *Anna* and they would say, well, you know she made a good portrayal of Anna, not realizing that I was very, very personal as well.

D: But it seems to me that is also running very close to danger in that it can be the quality of a bad actor. That it is always *his* personality we see; instead of seeing Hamlet we're seeing an actor called X. Because the better the actor, the more technical ability to produce Hamlet as opposed to putting his own thing in.

L: But the actor must fill the character which is written. Be an author's actor who submerges the *ego* in a role conceived in someone else's mind. The trick is not to play yourself in different disguises. The actor *must* put his own thing into it. Hamlet is not just putting on another nose, another voice. Olivier's Hamlet is very personal; and it was a technical masterpiece.

D: Why is it a technical masterpiece?

L: Because you thought of it as Hamlet, not as Olivier.

The reason for people saying that an actress has to be forty to play Juliet is that you have to understand what Juliet is all about. You must have lived it, you must have gone deep. Otherwise anyone younger would be better. Then there was only one way to do Hamlet. Then there was only one way to do anything, if you don't draw on personal experience. The danger lies, however, to go back to what we were talking about earlier, in that you *do* go sometimes through so much emotion onstage and use of your own experience that sometimes I think you can be confused offstage. Because the feeling of what is happening is so strong onstage. Sometimes the real life isn't equal. It is like living on fantasy, and not being able to cope with reality. If life onstage becomes so real because you really live it up there, it might create difficulties in the ordinary life, which doesn't demand all these emotions. And that can make it—because you are looking and searching all the time—somewhat shallow. There is a danger there.

D: Yeats wrote about a story known to the Noh players: "A young man was following a stately old woman through the streets of a Japanese town, and presently she turned to him and spoke: 'Why do you follow me?' 'Because you are so interesting.' 'That is not so, I am too old to be interesting.' But he wished, he told her, to become a player of old women on the Noh stage. If he would become famous as a Noh player, she said, he must not observe life, nor put on an old face and stint the music of his voice. He must know how to suggest an old woman and yet find it all in the heart."

L: That is what it is *all* about: suggest whatever character you're playing, and then find that character in your own heart. It is beautiful what he writes.

D: However, I remember also you describing your wandering down the street following a drunk to see how the drunk behaves.

L: Well, that doesn't defy what he says. Because I have to suggest it. You must know something. You must do that, too. But that is not what the man was doing, or that's not what she commented on. Also I am not saying following a drunk is necessarily right.

You know it is very strange, this acting. I know already I have started to play Judith Hearne on stage.* And

Ingmar was telling me—he is editing *The Serpent's Egg* and called yesterday—that there is one scene and it was not good, but he didn't have the heart to cut it out

---

*A producer had been discussing Liv Ullmann's starring in a film version of Brian Moore's *The Lonely Passion of Judith Hearne.*

because he said it was so typical of the me, the actress who wants to do everything, and it's much too much. And I know that scene was Anna Christie because it is what I try to do in the first act. And I'm not able to do it yet a year later. I know I was already thinking about Anna Christie. In the film it is just that I am walking into a room. I knew I was not going to get the front shot. I am to be very tired, and Ingmar said he has never seen any back so bowed, any feet so dragging. And I remember doing that scene and thinking this is a walk I must do for Anna Christie. It was bad for Ingmar's scene, but I was already preparing Anna. I have never really found it except the bowed shoulders. But I know I have started things now that are Judith Hearne. She—Anna—is talking to her hands all the time. Or to her purse. When she is really lost. She is suddenly commenting to her hands, which I think relates to Hearne, always having contact with her slippers. However, you can't do slippers in film except when the camera is set to move. But I think a very good way of portraying the loneliness of Judith Hearne is that she has this little thing, she communicates with her hands.

D: The little twinkle from her shoes?

L: Yes, the little buttons on her slippers that she looks down on and who look back at her like friendly twinkling eyes. But that is up to the director and photographers to show. If they don't really catch that, I lose those moments for Judith Hearne. But the hands I can control. I can always put them in focus in the film. And so Anna Christie has now already started to take on some of the habits of Judith Hearne. And that is what makes acting so very interesting to me. And that is why it's worth following a drunken man. Not that you imitate him necessarily as a drunk, but you can suddenly see something in him that gives you an insight. I know a lot about Judith Hearne, and I know my suggestion of loneliness by talking to the hands will work.

D: How do you cope with subtlety in film, which is very different from subtlety onstage?

L: Well, it's not that different. You just have to project a little bigger onstage, but it is the same reality. On film, you can have astonishment just in your eyes. Onstage maybe you must help it with your hands or a turn of the head, or something. But your facial expressions must always actually say the facial expression of the film—of life. Never more. Except in comedy. Never more. But, if you can, fill every pore.

Some actors say the theater is a big room and one has to play big. That is wrong. You mustn't play big; you must project but not get bigger and louder than life or the poor people in the first seats are lost.

D:   I hear that there is quite a bit of practical joking going on in this production among the actors.

L:   There is a lot. Just before we went onstage the other day someone said how good I was at disguising my private laughs in the first act and making them cries. So I put something in both my eyes today to come in with tears, and I put too much and couldn't open my eyes for five minutes. I sat onstage and the moment I opened them I saw Mary McCarty scratching her arm and I looked at her arm and I saw a big tattoo there. So I had to get up from the table so as not to laugh at that. It was very bad.

But this is an exceptionally long run for a dramatic play. So it's like giving a kind of revitalization to get through the evening. I can't explain it in another way. It's like giving yourself extra vitamin shots to go through something you already went through a hundred times. The repetition does take some of the reason away for doing a play.

D:   The reason to go through, I suppose, is for the same reason to go through it on the tenth or twentieth.

L:   Yes. Of course. You want to give a good performance. But it is *because* you want to give a good performance that you need something to pull yourself together. And if you don't get it by somebody giving you notes, telling what you're doing right or wrong, you try to pull yourself together artificially. Somebody drinks, we don't in this play, somebody takes shots, we don't in this play. We are trying to give each other a kind of shock to wake up and overcome and by overcoming concentrate more on the part. It does keep it alive. It won't keep it alive if it shows to the audience, of course, but it doesn't. Listen—this happens in all jobs—there comes a time when you must make a little fun of it to be able to go through it today and tomorrow and next month.

D:   You once said you felt actors had to dig into themselves in a more honest and cruel way—those are your words—than most people. Why?

L:   Because if they use themselves as their instrument it has to be nourished. You are your own instrument and you must use what is in you and put it into that character. To do Ophelia I find whatever madness there is in me and build on that. Whatever is my experience, build on that.

D:   In an interview which you did about *Scenes from a Marriage* you said, "Of course, we have emotional memories." That is Stanislavsky's phrase, and you have argued against his philosophy in the past.

L:   You must live with the emotional memories, and be very aware of them, but you cannot use just a memory and build a part on that. Stanislavsky actually says, try to remember when you cried here when your father died. And you can do that about ten times, but you can't do it anymore. But in the interview I meant that you must be constantly aware as much as you can of what you consist of. Both good and bad. You must know about the cruelty inside yourself when you're smiling very pleasantly. You must also be aware of the feeling of anger you have, because that feeling has an expression and that expression you can use. Whereas somebody who is not an actor can smile pleasantly and not be as aware of the other side of the mask. It is the same with a painter, an author, any creative artist. They have to be more cruel observers, both of themselves and of other people. Just as much of other people. It doesn't mean they love people less. But they do see the funny, or ironical, or even tragic parts of other people sometimes more clearly than people who are not forced to do that in their professions. Though it is not only in creative arts you start to look at people like this; I think, for example, doctors must, bartenders —oh, so many. Everybody really who has to deal with people.

D:   I thought you were making a point about actors especially. I thought that you were saying that you guys have to dig around in the garbage of your psyche to come up with—

L:   No, what I am talking about is true of any creative

person. But I don't think we dig consciously in life. That's where I don't agree with Stanislavsky. Because I don't think you can really dig consciously. Because when you take it out in the air it's of not the same value. You have used it up, in a way. You live very much in touch with your own feelings and with your own unconscious. Your unconscious is the real creator. If you ask Ingmar what his script is about he gets panicky. Because he doesn't really know how to put it in words other than those already in the script, and in the script are the words and the secrets. The unconscious. People who live very much in touch with their subconscious . . . It is not always pleasant, it doesn't make the best ground for living in harmony.

D:   We have talked a lot about interpretation. But aside from that, acting is also a lot of more simple things. Your voice and your body, you must have to work on improving their response.

L:   Oh, yes. Because my body is my instrument.

D:   "One of God's masterpieces," according to one critic.

L:   Thank you. I will frame it and show it to my grandchildren.

D:   Do you have coaches? Do you have people to show you something about dancing? Or something about voice?

L:   Oh, sure. Not regularly. But I have during all my life, which is one of the benefits of growing up in a repertory theater, being pushed into taking gymnastic classes, voice lessons, fencing, and singing, and all that. Fencing I was never good at. Gymnastics I've taken on and off. During this production I have done yoga. With my voice, I've worked for years and years. Because I have a problem with voice.

D:   Why?

L:   Well, I have an accent in Norway because I come from the north. I've tried to get rid of my accent. In Sweden I've had an accent because I came from Norway. In America I have an accent because I am not English. Only north in Norway do I speak correctly.

D:   You are talking about accent, a coach on dialect.

L:   It is more than that; your own language—your tone

—that is who you are—where you come from. One must be careful not to take out the nuances of speech in order to be perfect.

D:   Are you still working on that?

L:   I have stopped because I did it for such a long time with all kinds of teachers, and in the end I became too conscious of my voice and of my voice being a problem. Ingmar was one of the advisers saying I should leave my voice as it is.

D:   When you were doing *A Doll's House* and you had to dance the tarantella, could you do that or did you have to get somebody to coach?

L:   Of course I needed a coach. What do I know about tarantellas?

D:   If you were doing *A Doll's House* again would you be able to do it, or would you need another coach?

L:   I don't remember the steps from the tarantella. Anyway, every movement, every blocking is different from production to production.

D:   If you get into a musical you would get all sorts of advice?

L:   For that kind of thing, a director, a choreographer. There will be a singing teacher for the singing. You don't do it by yourself. Because those are things that are not part of your training. To sing or dance. That is doing things which are extended. An actor isn't supposed to have to dance the tarantella. It is like an artist who is going to paint Marie Antoinette when she is beheaded. He will have to seek some information about what she wore, if he wants it to be accurate. It is getting information about what you are doing.

To be a good theater actor you have to stay with the coaches. For example, Max von Sydow, who is a great actor, goes to a voice coach every day because he has been doing film for so many years, not theater. And now he is to do a play again, and must work on projecting. I saw a famous film star in *The Three Sisters*. I have no idea what she said; she spoke as if she were on the screen. Yet she is a wonderful actress.

D:   In *Face to Face*, when you did the scene where you're half crying and then you're laughing and crying, what are you doing there? Are you doing something completely technical?

L: It's very difficult to laugh. It's much easier to cry. Or to have the sound of crying. But you don't think of the technique while you do it; that belongs to your homework.

D: But that was really a technical accomplishment. It's not that you were actually putting yourself into the part.

L: In the case where I'm laughing? No. That isn't even my laughter. It just came out of my throat that way. But being rid of that technical problem—it took me years to know how to laugh and I still don't always know how to. But having learned it, I don't have to think about it, worry about it. I learned it. And then when that scene comes I don't have the stress that "Oh, I must make this sound like a laugh." Now the laugh comes like the cry comes. I can live in the scene. I'm free to make choices and I can laugh and cry without being stopped by technical limitations. For me, that scene in *Face to Face* was a great breakthrough.

D: I know a potter who spent sixteen years learning everything technical but he said that before he really became good he had to spend ten years forgetting. It is a similar freedom.

L: But I'm still being proud about it, right? It's the same as him only I have not forgotten yet. I'm still proud of being able to laugh. I need to get beyond that.

D: Ingmar wrote in his book about your ability to put feeling into any part of your body an extraordinary technical accomplishment. In *Persona* he asked you to put feeling into your lips? Right? And your lips get bigger.

L: It's a little romantic. I went to see *Persona* recently. I was waiting to see an enormous revelation on my lips. I couldn't see it.

D: You couldn't.

L: No.

D: Do you remember that incident?

L: I remember him saying it. I know he said it in the book about himself and as he was the one who said it,

I've always believed it to be true. I remember after he had seen the rushes—I lived with Bibi at the time—he phoned her. It was her scene. And he phoned her to say how wonderful she was. Then he said, "But I want you to tell Liv that half of the scene was hers. Because half of the story you're telling is showing in her face." And I do remember that because Bibi and I talked about it. But I couldn't see my lips grow.

D: But in the scene in *Face to Face,* when you're cracking up, what you are doing is a technical thing. There are no emotions?

L: Of course there are emotions. It's the same as everything we talked about: you let *her* emotions flow through you.

D: And if you had to do that scene every night on a stage for six months instead of once before a camera—it would be the same?

L: Yes. Sometimes better, sometimes worse. Again it has to do with inspiration because of the extra little thing. Doing too much or too little. Because I'm sure of the laughter—how to do the laughter—it wouldn't stop at that. But it would stop in the intensity of it. I wasn't using a trick or a private emotion in that scene. I wasn't thinking of anything, really. I was just sort of knowing that character and feeling open. I knew she was having a breakdown and was going to cry and laugh and I let it happen. That would have been the same onstage.

D: You said that film was in some ways more protective for an actress than the stage, and in other ways less protective.

L: It is more protective because you can redo it again and again until it is right. *But* once it's there, it's there for always. And you can't come the next day with a great inspiration and do it better.

When I saw *Persona*—you know, I hadn't seen it since it was made—there is a scene where I was to be very upset and I felt it was a wonderful trick of standing, waving a cigarette back and forth. I thought that would really show tension. Ingmar said, "Don't do it." And I was sure he was wrong. So I did it anyway, and thought that it was a wonderful idea. When I saw it the other day it looked so phony. Instead of seeing tension you are seeing an actress who is trying to show tension in a very banal way.

D: Most of the things that you criticize yourself on in earlier things are probably when you did too much.

L: It is almost always doing too much. That is my danger. I am more in danger of doing too much than too little.

D: That is curious because you are known for doing very little. *Time* wrote about how with the flick of an eyelash—

L: That is because Ingmar has, to a great extent, disciplined me and given me courage in myself. I don't have to do this thing with a cigarette. If I feel tension I trust it *will* show in my face and body. But if a director doesn't trust me and asks for more he'll get too much. I still don't know how to do the first act in *Anna Christie*. I do know that one out of thirty days I do it right. And then for twenty-nine I do too much. I'm still really working on it. She is exhausted. She should be sitting at one place, but I'm up and going all the time. I've no reason to move. Okay, she is nervous. But still, there is no— It's not in the lines. José gave me a wonderful blocking, only I cannot fill it. It's not his fault, it's my limitations. I'm always better when I don't move too much.

D: Do you think that people are more likely to be swept away into the part in watching a movie, or watching a play?

L: In the best moments, I think a play. Because they are breathing together with the performers. They know it's happening here and now, and they can feel their own participation. Also because in a film you're always aware of the camera and you don't zoom in on what you want to watch. In the theater you make your own choices.

D: You said that you try to put Jenny into Liv and through Liv let Jenny come out. Isn't that almost what is happening with the audience? Mr. Smith is sitting in the audience, and if it really works he will allow Anna to go into Mr. Smith and through Mr. Smith come out.

L: That is what I have said: it becomes Liv and it becomes Anna and it becomes Mr. Smith.

D: I still am not convinced it isn't just two people—Mr. Smith and Anna.

L: It's a very subtle thing. There are actors that are so masked that you don't see them. For them that is good, it is their big talent. To disappear in a character. Other actors' big talent is to use themselves, to let the character come out of what they are.

D: But the character has to come out of the actor whether the actor—

L: There are actors who put papier-mâché noses on and they're wonderful and there are actors who never do. You identify more closely *when* you see Laurence Olivier, and he is really using his naked eye, *than* when he's doing Richard III and you are marveling at the details of his hunchback and everything.

D: Let's take the day you did Nora better than you had ever done Nora before, you really thought it was a perfect performance, right? Did they think it is Nora, or did they think it's partly Nora and partly Liv Ullmann.

L: No, they think it is Nora. But they also know it is me. They have the fantasy. They have the fantasy and they've shared it with me. That's the wonderful thing. They've shared it with somebody.

D: Isn't fantasy being fooled?

L: No. Fantasy is something I believe in completely. And identify with completely. When my daughter is playing with her toy animals she knows they are her toy animals, but the wonderful thing is that they are all totally alive to her. She has to put them all to bed. She has the knowledge they are toys but at the same time she allows them to be alive.

D: Well, at least you are consistent: I remember you once said it's not make-believe, what I am doing up there. I'm not *cheating*.

L: Yes. As the observed it's real. As the observer I know it's me. And us doing it. Together. With the audience. As the observer they think it's them, when in the best moment they identify, and at the same time they have the experience of being observed.

D: When the anger of Anna Christie is there in act three you can still be in and out of it so very, very quickly—aware that the lighting has changed, for example.

L: Yes, because *personally* I don't feel anything. I'm not lost in my own feelings.

D: I remember when seeing rushes of *The Abdication* and you would be doing a scene and then they'd say, "Cut." And the camera always goes another few frames and suddenly you—Liv—are there. The second the cut comes you are right out of the part and have become the actress.

L: It's important for me not to be lost in the character. It's important for me to relate, "This is business, let's come back to what we want to achieve here." So I almost do it demonstratively to detach myself immediately. And recharge.

D: Much of what you have been saying is that the interpretation must come from the heart—the center of gravity.

L: Which also bears out the difficulty. I am always fighting. If the true sense of acting really belongs to the discovery of the soul of another person, can we ever completely find it? Because whose hearts and whose souls can be captured? The search is always disturbed by other things.

D: But when you're *thinking* of the part, I mean, not on the stage but when you're working out who that is, you *know*.

L: It's an unconscious thing.

D: That's right.

L: And that is where I think one should let it stay. You are dealing with something so fragile, something inside yourself, that explaining it is almost impossible. But if the interpretation has gone through something real within me, at least what I do will be closer to truth. The goal is the impossible. It is the cloth weaving the cloth, it is Anna being Anna, and it never happens but you can come close to it at moments.

D: And that is something that comes out of training or is it from living?

L: I think it is really closer to living than to training, but of course it has to do with training, too. Working on

your body and voice. But you must be so well trained, for such a long time, that you don't think about it any longer. So that it is a natural state for you to talk loud, for example. To talk loud even if the true feeling is low. You must have no consciousness and total consciousness at the same time, which is a contradiction: at the same time you're dealing with your own soul you are dealing with how to *express* it, *translate* it to an audience. Without them being aware that you are *working*. If they sense that there on the stage someone is *pretending* to show their naked soul, and because of the pretense they feel *cheated*, you have *failed*.

You know, it is difficult to cheat a child. They will always sense it.

D: Do you think children are more perceptive to phoniness?

L: Oh, yes.

D: They are without self-consciousness. It is like when a child first paints things, there's no consciousness then.

L: I would call it innocence—a pure soul. You said that to me once before: A tree is that black dot with all the red things around it, and not before ten people have told the child that trees don't look like that does he look at his dots and never paint again.

D: The Japanese used to make oil plates which had a lovely design and yet were very, very inexpensive. Just a willow tree made with a few soft strokes of pigment to form the decoration. Because these plates cost almost nothing, children were used to paint the design. The great potters say today that adults could not make that. They would never have the freedom or innocence to just do a tree as two lines.

L: Because the soul isn't clean anymore.

D: But how does one get back to a clean soul?

L: I don't know, I'm not back. But I feel I am closer to it. My problem in life is that my innocence and my naiveté work against me. But it also happens to be my strength. Because I am in touch with something inside me that many people are not that close to—even if they might be wiser and more read and more adjusted to life than I am. Partly, I think it comes from solitude, being an islander, so to speak. I think solitude—and loneliness—in some ways can be good for an artist. Even a sense of rejection. It makes you establish your own growth.

D:    So what advice do you give to a young man or woman who wants to act? Don't go watch old women in the streets, young man, you have to know it all in your heart. What does he have to do?

L:    He can try being more human, which is something naive now, because of the way I'm saying it. But he has to— What Yeats means is don't *watch* her, *feel* her. See ten women but instead of observing, be part of them, feel them, be sensitive to who they are, why they are. Try to put yourself into them. Read from them what they are about. Don't watch a gesture and go and imitate it. Find out what is behind that gesture. Identify.

D:    Why do you think that is naive?

L:    Because I always talk about it. I see something—an image, a face, a gesture—and I think . . . I want to remember this because I feel I can explain it. I always say that the most important thing to me as an actress is to be human. And then I'm afraid I'm not really human either, because I'm working all the time. But I think that maybe what I mean is *I want to keep that quality alive, and the feeling, even if I can't use it anywhere else than on the stage.* That quality of unspoken, nondescribed observation, caring, interest of another human being—as well as myself.

D:    That isn't naive. You have expressed something profound about who you are.

L:    It can't be that profound if I've said it.

D:    You are saying something very significant about yourself.

L:    I've said it in a different way just now and I haven't really known before what I've meant—because it belies my whole life. "The most important thing for me is to be a human being." And then: What kind of human being?

Always getting tense and working and watching people? But I think maybe you can be a human being in your *art*. And part of being a human being can mean just that. If it is something you *give*, even if as a *person* you can't give it, maybe that is what *acting* is about: to be able to identify and share what people who see you can immediately identify with. Because they recognize it. Because they have identified it before in somebody else, or within themselves. It is also recognizing who is there *onstage*. It is Liv doing her human life.

D:    A final question. I believe that the Mr. Smith that flies in from Chicago and is taken to the theater is identifying with the loneliness, the sense of rejection, the frustration of lost love or whatever Anna Christie is. And the fact that he identifies with it is the extent into which you make it work. Why does it work? How do you reduce five days of action into two hours or three hours of real-life sobbing into forty seconds—which is what you're allowed before the next scene?

L:    Actors can do it because they have very exact staging, or training. Unfortunately, theater also has bad actors who feel they have to do something *all the time*. They're reacting to everything—jumping, screaming—and it becomes clouded. It looks good, oh, this man is alive, or whatever, but it's not really good. If you have *few* selected reactions, you can allow for quietness. And you give room for the audience to fill in the quietness with their own interpretation. If I don't do things all the time, they do things for me. That *they* have believed in. They can make bridges to the stage as well as the other way around.

D:    Which is almost saying what Charlie Parker said: the audience is letting the character play them.

L:    Isn't it strange how everything comes down to the same thing? Even the opposites meet: Charlie Parker, Yeats. Somewhere they meet. The true things meet. We may never reach Truth. But we can come close to it. Also, in life, if you respect the integrity of your human fellow friend, a bridge of understanding will be there between you, and being together here will be an embrace instead of a rejection.

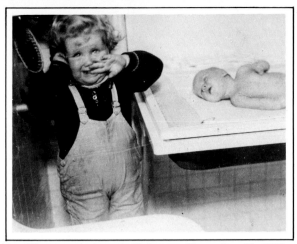

Liv Ullmann was born in Tokyo on December 16, 1938. This first picture of her is at age six weeks, with her older sister, Bitten.

With her father and Bitten on Lake Simco, outside Toronto, where the family had moved. Winter of 1940.

In Canada, summer of 1940.

On the train from Los Angeles to San Francisco, 1941, with her father, mother, and sister. Liv Ullmann is three.

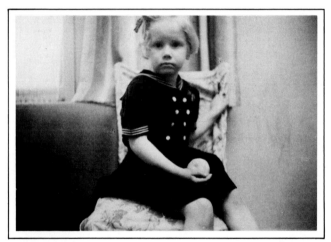

1942.

Again with Bitten, September 1943.

Confirmation, 1953.

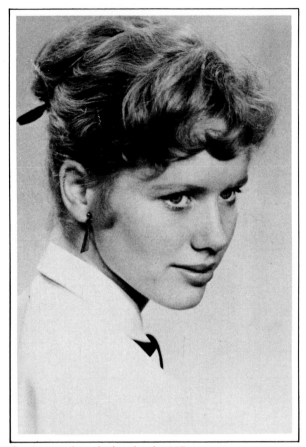

Graduation from high school, 1957.

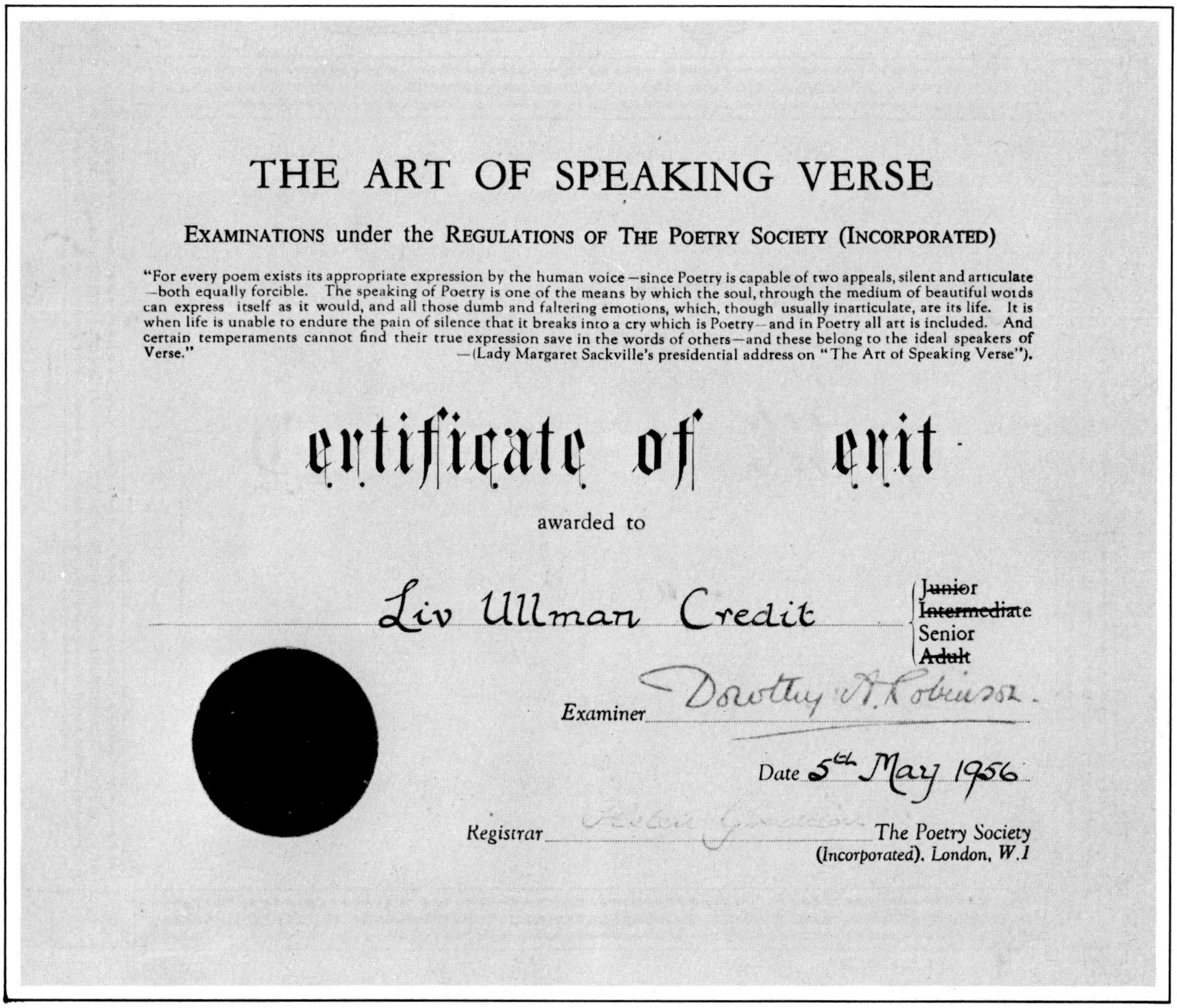

# THE ART OF SPEAKING VERSE

### EXAMINATIONS under the REGULATIONS OF THE POETRY SOCIETY (INCORPORATED)

"For every poem exists its appropriate expression by the human voice—since Poetry is capable of two appeals, silent and articulate—both equally forcible. The speaking of Poetry is one of the means by which the soul, through the medium of beautiful words can express itself as it would, and all those dumb and faltering emotions, which, though usually inarticulate, are its life. It is when life is unable to endure the pain of silence that it breaks into a cry which is Poetry—and in Poetry all art is included. And certain temperaments cannot find their true expression save in the words of others—and these belong to the ideal speakers of Verse." —(Lady Margaret Sackville's presidential address on "The Art of Speaking Verse").

## ertificate of erit

awarded to

*Liv Ullman Credit*

Junior
~~Intermediate~~
Senior
~~Adult~~

Examiner *Dorothy A. Robinson*

Date *5th May 1956*

Registrar _____

The Poetry Society
(Incorporated), London, W.1

39

Beginning moments are rarely known to the outsider. What is seen is the later culmination of success. But always, for everyone, there are the beginning moments.

Liv Ullmann's first appearance on the public stage occurred in Trondhjem when she was eleven and played an orphan in a play by Elsa Beskow. This was followed at age twelve when she played a bluebell in *The Flower Story* also by Elsa Beskow, a play about vegetables and flowers.

Five years pass. School days. Then comes the first adult chance: member of the chorus in *Jomfru Hook von Holland*. (No picture exists to record that moment.) Next comes a minor role as a maid in *Charmøren* by Finn Bøe (right). Once successes become apparent it is easy for critics to give plaudits; much more discerning was the reviewer who wrote of this 1957 play: "Bewitching is the blond Liv Ullmann who will soon throw off her maid's gown in the art of acting."

Her next opportunity was in Stavanger, the play *Det Lykkelige Valg*, where she plays "a girl." In the picture below from that production she can be seen with scrutiny at left rear.

Production: ***Fjols til Fjells (Fools in the Mountains)***
Director: **Edith Carlmar**
Premiere: **Oslo, September 15, 1957**

Otto Carlmar produced a number of Norwegian films which his wife directed. They are simple romances and were noted by his preference for young, shapely girls whom he costumed in skimpy—and sometimes no—clothing. In *Fjols til Fjells* he cast Liv Ullmann in her first film role. It was a minor part—young girl at a ski lodge. She appears only twice: in the scene pictured here, and later, showing an inviting hip on a staircase.

Nonetheless, it was a beginning, and Carlmar took some publicity shots of his new starlet.

Today, Otto Carlmar is an old man living in an Oslo apartment building. In his files are dozens of old Scandinavian magazines, most of them no longer published, featuring his starlet become star. Liv Ullmann in color, in gravure; looking sweet, looking alluring; on the cover of one provocatively biting into a large red apple.

Production: **The Diary of Anne Frank, adapted by Frances Goodrich and Albert Hackett**
Character: **Anne Frank**
Director: **Aud Richter**
Premiere: **Stavanger, 1957/58 repertory season**

Anne Frank was the first lead part for the girl who had a year earlier been turned down by acting school. It brought success, a contract for $600 a year. Had Liv Ullmann been unable to portray that tragic young girl nothing else in this book would have been quite the same.

It was, however, a happy beginning as she recalls:

"A train left the Oslo station on its way to Stavanger. She was eighteen, sparkling with happiness—now at last it was going to happen! Securely tucked away in her handbag was a stage contract, already grubby from being continually admired, from fingers that opened and refolded it again and again. Shown to everyone who asked to see it—also to many who didn't."

Production: **Karrusel, by Alex Brinchmann**
Character: **Sister Jenny**
Director: **Gisle Straume**
Premiere: **Stavanger, 1957/58 repertory season**

Production: **You Can't Take It with You, by Moss Hart and George S. Kaufman**
Character: **Alice**
Director: **Bjørn Endresson**
Premiere: **Stavanger, 1957/58 repertory season**

*Karrusel* and *You Can't Take It with You*, together with *Anne Frank*, comprised Liv Ullmann's first season onstage. In some of these photographs from the productions one is aware of a teenage actress; but in others it is a surprise to realize that they were taken more than twenty years ago.

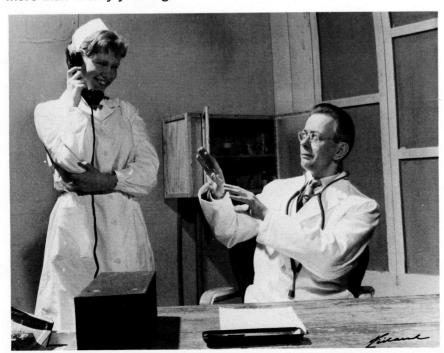

Production: *Hamlet,* by William Shakespeare
Character: **Ophelia**
Director: **Bjørn Endresson**
Premiere: **Stavanger, 1958/59 repertory season**

Liv Ullmann was only twenty when she played Ophelia. It is often commented about Juliet—in fact, Liv has said it herself—that the actress portraying the girl of thirteen will have had to absorb a great deal more than thirteen years usually gives a person. The same statement can be made about Ophelia.

"I loved the mad scene, but it would be more interesting today. However, it is not a play that I would like to do, as I feel a constriction in the elegance of the verse of Shakespeare. But I would find much more in the part than I did then."

Production: **Insektliv (Insect Life), by Josef and Karel Čapek**
Character: **First pupa**
Director: **Bjarne Andersen**
Premiere: **Stavanger, 1958/59 repertory season**
No picture exists.

Production: **Look Homeward, Angel, by Thomas Wolfe, adapted by Ketti Frings**
Character: **A guest at the Dixieland Hotel**
Director: **Gerda Ring**
Premiere: **Stavanger, 1958/59 repertory season**

Production: **Kristin Lavransdatter, by Sigrid Undset, adapted by Tormod Skagestad**
Character: **Kristin**
Director: **Bjarne Andersen**
Premiere: **Stavanger, 1958/59 repertory season**

The adaptation of *Kristin Lavransdatter* was very successful. In addition to the Stavanger production, it was staged with a different cast in Oslo, where it ran for several hundred performances; it also toured. The author of the adaptation, Tormod Skagestad, is director of the Norwegian Theater in Oslo, where Liv Ullmann played for several seasons after the Stavanger years. He was also the director of the Broadway production of *A Doll's House,* starring Ullmann in 1975.

Production: **_Ung Flukt (Young Escape)_**
Director: **Edith Carlmar**
Premiere: **Oslo, October 8, 1959**

Lead role in a film at nineteen.

_Ung Flukt_ gathers dust in a film archive, as it should. It comes to life in the mind, however, as a minor milestone in the career of an actress. True to producer Otto Carlmar's formula, the clothing is scanty and, in one lakeside scene which shocked some of the Ullmann family, nonexistent.

Production: ***Flyktningen (The Fugitive),***
   ***by Fritz Hockwålder***
Character: **The wife**
Director: **Bjarne Andersen**
Premiere: **Stavanger, 1959/60 repertory season**

"*Flyktningen* is a play I remember I enjoyed doing because it was my first part where I was not playing a young girl. Instead of depending on that kind of youthful vitality, I had to be mature, and it demanded something new of me."

Production: ***The Pretenders,* by Henrik Ibsen**
Character: **Margrete**
Director: **Toralf Sandø**
Premiere: **Stavanger, 1959/60 repertory season**

Production: **Mannen som kom (The Man Who Came),**
         **by Ugo Betti**
Character: **Silvia**
Director: **Gerhard Knoop**
Premiere: **Trondhjem, October 6, 1960; Oslo,**
         **February 7, 1961**

Production: **The Process Against Jesus,**
         **by Diego Fabbri**
Character: **Virgin Mary**
Director: **Bjarne Andersen**
Premiere: **Oslo, September 10, 1961**

*The Man Who Came* was Ullmann's debut in Oslo as a leading lady. It is a very dramatic play, and she remembers having great fun doing it. It is the story of a man who arrives at the house of three women. He lusts after all of them, including the daughter. When her mother discovers this, she sends him down a well for water and then removes the rope, killing him. *The Process Against Jesus* was her next production. Both plays were staged at the Norwegian Theater, which was her artistic home for almost five years.

During these years, Liv Ullmann lived in Oslo with her husband, Dr. Hans Jacob Stang, a psychiatrist, and their dog, Pet. Pet, with a malleable sense of allegiance, spent her later years with Ingmar Bergman on Fårö.

54

Production: ***Tonny***
Character: **Kari**
Director: **Nils Müller**
Premiere: **Oslo, January 22, 1962**

Production: **The Caucasian Chalk Circle,**
     **by Bertolt Brecht**
Character: **Grusha**
Director: **Peter Palitzsch**
Premiere: **Oslo, January 14, 1962**

In the career of any creative artist there come moments of significant maturation and/or change. These are relatively easy to recognize in some fields. A painter, a potter, a composer leave signs in his or her work that identify the metamorphosis. Unfortunately, these moments are almost impossible to discern in a performing artist from static representations of the work. In the interview "On Acting" in this book, it is apparent that *every new production*—even the contemplation of a future part—stirs its own new chemistry of change. Nonetheless, there have been occasions within Liv Ullmann's career as actress where some basic new equipment of experience has been added to the art form. Certainly the vista opened by the responsibility of the leading role *(Anne Frank)* must have been one. Later, the theatrical omniscience of Ingmar Bergman, the victory over the Hollywood modus (in *The Abdication),* the resolution of technique in *Face to Face,* and the realization, in *The Human Voice,* of that distant place "where illusion and reality meet" can be noted as occasions.

The production of *The Caucasian Chalk Circle* was also one:

When I was twenty-two, Peter Palitzsch, a German director, came to our theater in Oslo. . . . He taught me that everything we portray on the stage ought to be shown from two sides. Be illustrated in both black and white. When I smile, I must also show the grimace behind it. Try to depict the countermovement—the counteremotion.

I learned to work more consciously.

I remember the opening scene of the *Chalk Circle.* At the first reading I thought I was to play a woman in a heroic situation. Her name was Grusha.

Revolution had come to the village where she lived in poverty. Everyone had fled the murder and fire that followed in the wake of war. While she herself was running away she found an infant abandoned by its mother. She stopped without knowing what she would do with the little bundle wrapped in silk and velvet, precious materials that she had never touched before.

My interpretation was to sit down and look tenderly and softly at the baby. Sing to it, pick it up, and take it with me.

"Think a bit deeper," the director said. "Show her doubts: surely she must have had some? Her cowardice: don't you feel it? And what about her ambivalence in the face of this new responsibility? The audience will sympathize with you

anyway. Even if they don't grasp everything you are trying to illustrate, they will recognize you as acting in a way
they themselves might have acted. No spontaneous nobility.
Not necessarily symbolizing goodness all the time."

My interpretation became this:

The woman is sitting with the baby, but puts it down as she
realizes what a hindrance it will be on her flight. She stands
up and walks away. Stops. Doubt. Turns back. Reluctantly
sits down again. Looks at the little bundle. Looks away. Then,
finally, she picks it up with a gesture of resignation and runs
on. . . .

I, who for years had kept Stanislavsky's book on the art of
acting on my bedside table, now began to look for other
ways.

Partly, I found a new technique which seemed right for
me. . . . Less feelings, more concentration on giving expression to the feelings.

Production: ***Kort är Sommaren (Summer Is Short)***
Character: **Eva**
Director: **Bjarne Henning-Jensen**
Premiere: **Sweden, 1962**

Although the title does not indicate it, this Swedish film is an adaptation of Knut Hamsun's *Pan*. Edvarda was played by Bibi Andersson. It was the first time the two actresses had met. They became close friends and have remained so.

Production: ***Burning Darkness*, by Antonio Buero Vallejo**
Character: **Juana**
Director: **Pål Skjønberg**
Premiere: **Oslo, March 2, 1962**

*Burning Darkness* takes place in a boardinghouse for the blind. The residents there have learned to live in harmony with their blindness until the arrival of a new boy. His anger at being blind spreads to others, ultimately replacing harmony with death.

"It was a wonderful, wonderful part to play," recalls Liv Ullmann. "During rehearsal, before we went into what the play was about, we spent a lot of time concentrating on the image of being blind. Initially, we thought of researching it by going to a home for blind people, but we didn't. We had all seen blind people and we used our fantasy to find our characters. We also did a lot of rehearsals in blindfolds, where we learned how you react differently to people who speak to you, to noises, to everything if you cannot communicate with your eyes. It was a wonderful experience as an actress because you were forced to use your tools in a different way. It's one of my favorite plays."

(Burning Darkness)

61

Production: *Peer Gynt*, by Henrik Ibsen
Character: **Solveig**
Director: **Tormod Skagestad**
Premiere: **Oslo, September 3, 1962**

Production: *Medmenneske (Fellow Being),*
**by Olav Duun**
Character: **Ragnhild**
Director: **Knut Hergel**
Premiere: **Kristiansand, January 2, 1963; Oslo,
January 8, 1963**

Production: *Ungen (The Child),* by Oskar Braaten
Character: **Milja**
Director: **Jack Fjeldstad**
Premiere: **Oslo, February 5, 1963**

*Ungen* is set in Oslo and based on a true situation earlier in the city's history. The story centers on Milja, who has had an illegitimate child. There was a woman in those days whose house was open to any unmarried women with children. She spent her days tending the babies while the mothers worked and her evenings persuading them to come home and not go out with new boy friends. Milja, unhappy and depressed by her situation, goes to a bar and gets drunk; the authorities take away her child. The woman explains to the officials that the barroom scene was an accident and regains the possession of the child. She returns home with it, and then says to Milja that she has one hour to make a commitment to keep the child before the authorities come again to claim it.

The two pictures on the next pages show the dramatic change of emotions that come over Milja. Without makeup. The first is taken as she nurses her baby; the second while she is protecting it from the officials.

Production: ***Puntila*, by Bertolt Brecht**
Character: **Eva**
Director: **Peter Palitzsch**
Premiere: **Oslo, March 6, 1964**

*Puntila* was the last play Liv Ullmann was to perform at the Norwegian Theater for almost ten years. Following this production she moved to the National Theater.

*Puntila,* as staged by Peter Palitzsch, was played with more comedy than is normally given the lines. Liv Ullmann was playing Eva, the farmer's daughter.

The photographs from this production are interesting: they show Eva assuming several different postures within the course of the play: from innocent to sophisticate, farmer's daughter to lady. Although Liv Ullmann was twenty-five when she played in *Puntila,* in the first picture, at least, she looks barely half of that.

Production: *Faust,* by Johann Wolfgang von Goethe
Character: **Margarete**
Director: **Jørn Ording**
Premiere: **Oslo, September 5, 1963**

Production: ***Romeo and Juliet,*** by William Shakespeare
Character: **Juliet**
Director: **Per Bronken**
Premiere: **Oslo, October 8, 1964**

Production: **Saint Joan, by George Bernard Shaw**
Character: **Joan of Arc**
Director: **Arild Brinchmann**
Premiere: **Oslo, January 28, 1965**

The four productions that follow were all filmed for Norwegian television.

Production: **The Crucible, by Arthur Miller**
Character: **Mary Warren**
Director: **Knut M. Hansson**
Premiere: **Norwegian television, August 31, 1965**

Production: **The Trigon, by James Broom Lynne**
Character: **Mabel**
Director: **Arne Thomas Olsen**
Premiere: **Norwegian television, May 5, 1966**

Production: ***The Cocktail Party,*** **by T. S. Eliot**
Character: **Celia Coplestone**
Director: **Michael Elliot**
Premiere: **Norwegian television, September 5, 1967**

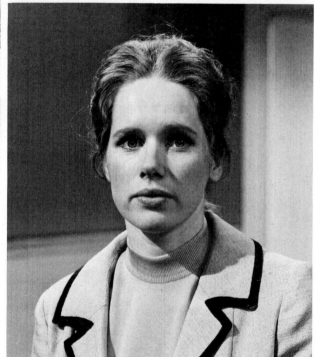

Production: ***Uncle Vanya,*** **by Anton Chekhov**
Character: **Sonja**
Director: **Gerhard Knoop**
Premiere: **Norwegian television, September 26, 1963**

Production: **De Kalte Ham Skarven (They Called Him Skarven)**
Character: **Ragna**
Director: **Erik Folke Gustavson**
Premiere: **Oslo, February 4, 1965**

*Skarven* is Norwegian for "cormorant," a fish-eating diving sea bird. It is also the name given to a fisherman on his first solo trip to the fishing grounds. This helps to make the title slightly less melodramatic. It does not help the film, however, which is represented here.

In the Norwegian Film Institute high up on a dusty, ignored shelf sit the moth-eaten remains of a stuffed cormorant; and it, in turn, is what remains of the film.

The timing of *Skarven*'s release is ironical. Onstage, Liv Ullmann has been a triumphant success in Brecht, and concurrently in Shaw's *Saint Joan*. *Skarven* represents the nadir of her film life.

The photograph at the top of the page was taken in the spring of 1965. The star of the National Theater is sitting, accompanied by Pet, by the melting snow. She has just returned from a trip to Stockholm and a meeting with Ingmar Bergman to discuss the part she is about to play in *Persona*.

Turning to the next page, we move into a new chapter in the life—both professional and private—of Liv Ullmann.

Production:        ***Persona***
Character:        **Elizabeth Vogler**
Director:        **Ingmar Bergman**
Swedish premiere:        **October 18, 1966**

In reviewing *Scenes from a Marriage*, many critics observed that, as the film was originally made for television, Bergman had used close-ups to take advantage of the medium's strength. This is a facile judgment because the close-up dominates all his films featuring Liv Ullmann: *Persona, Hour of the Wolf, The Passion of Anna, The Shame, Cries and Whispers, Scenes from a Marriage, Face to Face, The Serpent's Egg,* and *Autumn Sonata.*

In many of these films the so-called story line is minimal, plot is secondary. The beginnings, middles, and endings are, in a way, all centers. These centers invariably have to do with internal battles and resolutions within the characters' minds. It would be pedantic and—worse—probably inaccurate to attempt a description of the moments caught in these photographs. For those who have seen these films the photographs can evoke a memory of a scene on the screen. For anyone, they are a glimpse into the relationship between director and actress.

Liv Ullmann has written of Ingmar Bergman's use of the camera:

I love close-ups. To me they are a challenge. The closer a camera comes, the more eager I am to show a completely naked face, show what is behind the skin, the eyes; inside the head. Show the thoughts that are forming.

To work with Ingmar is to go on a journey of discovery within my own self. To be able to realize all the things I dreamed of as a girl.

Discard the mask and show what is behind it.

The camera comes so close—and there is much of myself that is captured.

Closer to the audience than in any other medium—the human being is shown on the screen.

The camera meets me more exposed than the lover who thinks he has read my thoughts.

Even when I tell myself that I am expressing a role, I can never completely hide who *I* am, what *I* am.

The audience, at the moment of identification, meets a person, not a role, not an actress.

A face which confronts them directly:

This is what I know about women. This is what *I* have experienced, have seen. This is what I want to share.

It is no longer a question of make-up, of hair, of beauty.

It is an exposure that goes way beyond.

Of course, three elements are at work: placement of the camera hard against the face, the character described in Bergman's script, and the actress's interpretation.

While it is true that the title of this book, *Without Makeup,* is legitimized by the whole career of Liv Ullmann—the average housewife leaving for the super-

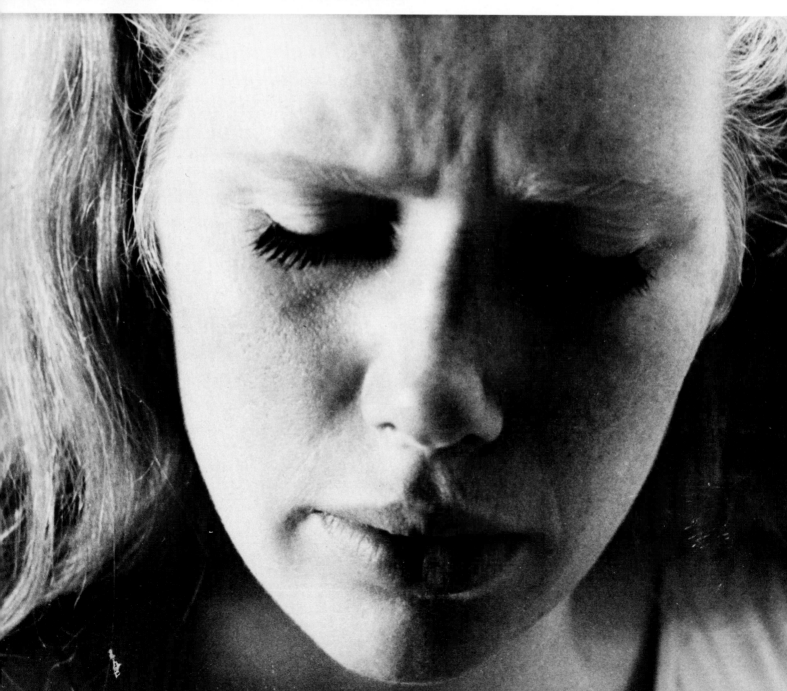

SNÅ LEKKATIRATER PÅ FARÖ SONRAR 1965 i AUGUSTI

NO

market uses more—it is not that Liv Ullmann presents her face scrubbed clean that ultimately is interesting; it is that she has learned how to allow the emotion behind the thought to become the real makeup. It is as if she somehow has been able to scrape the anguish, hope, love, despair from within—from that strange complex of mind, heart, and stomach nerves—to adorn the visage with that makeup-reality. "Makeup" and "real-ity" should be contradictory terms, but in this context they are fused. The credit for this accomplishment must lie with the actress, but in film it first surfaces in her collaboration with Bergman. This Brobdingnagian leap in technique will not be equaled until *The Human Voice* when, through a new mastery, she is able to command *onstage* the audience's unerring focus on her face.

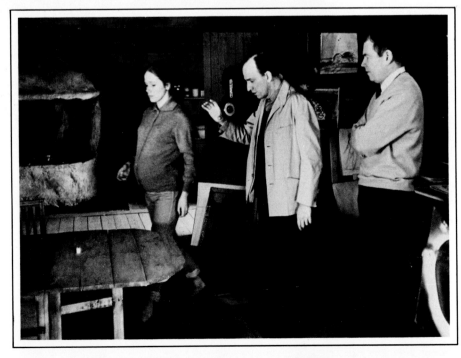

The pictures on these and the next two pages were all taken during the shooting of *Hour of the Wolf*. Before the film was finished, Linn, daughter of Bergman and Ullmann, was born. Upon returning to the set the actress wore a pillow to maintain a consistent profile.

Production:      *Hour of the Wolf*
Character:       **Alma**
Director:        **Ingmar Bergman**
Swedish premiere: **February 19, 1968**

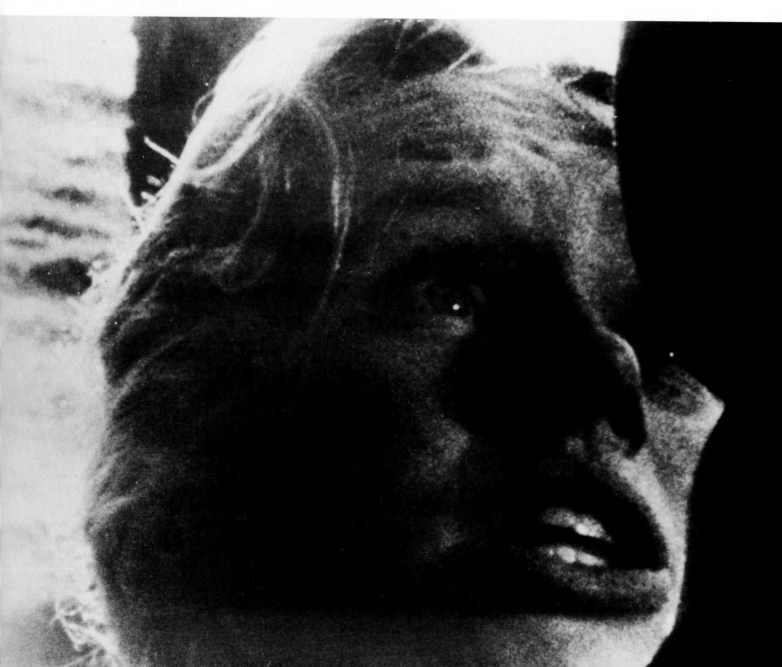

Production: **Quinder, Kvinder, Kvinner,**
**by Sandra Key-Åberg**
Characters: **Various**
Director: **Aloysius Valente**
Premiere: **Oslo, November 12, 1966**

This play, which opened three months after Linn was born, is a series of sketches of different women. Some of the pieces were cabaret in nature, others more serious. In one skit Ullmann plays the part of a reluctant widow, a part to be recalled twelve years later in rehearsing the widow Madame Popova in *The Bear*. The second sketch is about a group of "women for Peace" who are always more concerned with cocktail parties and costumes than with the cause they are championing.

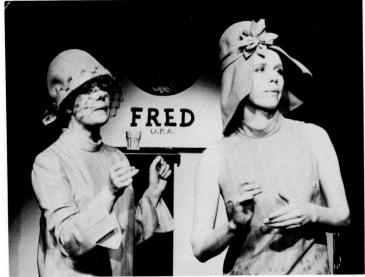

Production: **Anne Pedersdatter, by H. Wiers-Jensen**
Character: **Anne**
Director: **Knut Hergel**
Premiere: **Oslo, January 19, 1967**

This well-known Scandinavian play is about a woman who is burned as a witch after being accused of making her old husband die because she is in love with his son.

At night, Liv Ullmann played Anne; during the daytime she rehearsed *Six Characters in Search of an Author*.

Production: ***Six Characters in Search of an Author,***
              **by Luigi Pirandello**
Character: **Stepdaughter**
Director: **Ingmar Bergman**
Premiere: **Oslo, April 1, 1967**

The production of *Six Characters* was widely acclaimed in Oslo. Liv Ullmann also recalls it as a wonderful experience:

"Ingmar made what you were doing very important. Going to the rehearsal you were made part of an artistic, controlled world; and there were no limits to what we felt the director would let us do.

"I had one great difficulty: at that time I did not know how to laugh effectively onstage. Ingmar was really driving me: this part will not work if you are not able to give a big, one-minute, from-the-stomach laugh. Everyone was giving me advice on how to get the laugh. In my car driving home from the theater I was like a madwoman rehearsing this wild laugh. What people driving past must have thought I don't know."

The first two photographs are from rehearsal, the last is from the actual production.

*(Six Characters in Search of an Author)*

Production: **An-Magritt**
Character: **An-Magritt**
Director: **Arne Skouen**
Premiere: **Norway, 1968**

An-Magritt was a seventeenth-century Norwegian girl created by the twentieth-century novelist Johan Falkberget. She is an illiterate orphan who, in the face of a destiny that seems bleak, struggles and in the end stands triumphant as a proof to other unfortunates that there is hope. An-Magritt is still a heroine today, and bookstores do brisk business in the novel.

(An-Magritt)

Production: ***The Shame***
Character: **Eva Rosenberg**
Director: **Ingmar Bergman**
Swedish premiere: **September 29, 1968**

Max von Sydow is an actor who has worked for many years with Ingmar Bergman, both onstage and as part of the Bergman "repertory" film group. He appeared with Liv Ullmann in *Hour of the Wolf, The Shame, The Passion of Anna,* and later in Jan Troell's *The Emigrants* and *The New Land*. Discussing him recently, Liv Ullmann said, "He is a friend I love dearly as perhaps you can only love someone you have both worked with and known personally. It is a double relationship mixed into one. We haven't worked together for several years and I miss that very much."

(The Shame)

Production: *The Passion of Anna*
Character: **Anna Fromm**
Director: **Ingmar Bergman**
Swedish premiere: **November 10, 1969**

Production: **Cold Sweat**
  Director: **Terence Young**
  Premiere: **Unknown**

*Cold Sweat* shows up on television periodically. It is not bad vintage Bronson, but it certainly is not a good film. It was Liv Ullmann's first opportunity to act after her long personal relationship with Bergman had ended.

Production: **The Night Visitor**
  Character: **Esther Jenks**
  Director: **Laslo Benedek**
  Premiere: **New York, February 10, 1971**

Like *Cold Sweat,* this film was made at a time when Liv Ullmann's private life was painful. Although *The Night Visitor* received some laudatory reviews, it was, on the whole, loudly panned. It is hard to understand how this psychological thriller could have turned out so badly in the hands of such talent: Laslo Benedek, director (*The Wild One* and *Death of a Salesman*); Max von Sydow and Liv Ullmann from the Bergman ensemble; and Trevor Howard.

Production: ***Britannicus,* by Jean Racine**
Character: **Junia**
Director: **Edith Roger**
Premiere: **Oslo, February 20, 1971**

*Britannicus,* performed at the National Theater, was Liv Ullmann's first stage production in four years, and the first since her breakup with Bergman. The stage has often been for her a refuge from moments of despair in private life. Unfortunately, it failed her this time.

"I hated every moment of it. It was awful. I had returned to Norway and this play made me leave again. They used the fact of Ingmar's and my films for the promotion, then they gave me this part of a weeping little ingénue. It is the worst part you can have, even as a little girl, because it's not acting—just symbolizing innocence. I was thirty-two and wanted to show other things than an eighteen-year-old. I hated it. I hated every moment of it, and when I got an offer to do a film again outside Norway—*Pope Joan*—I took it."

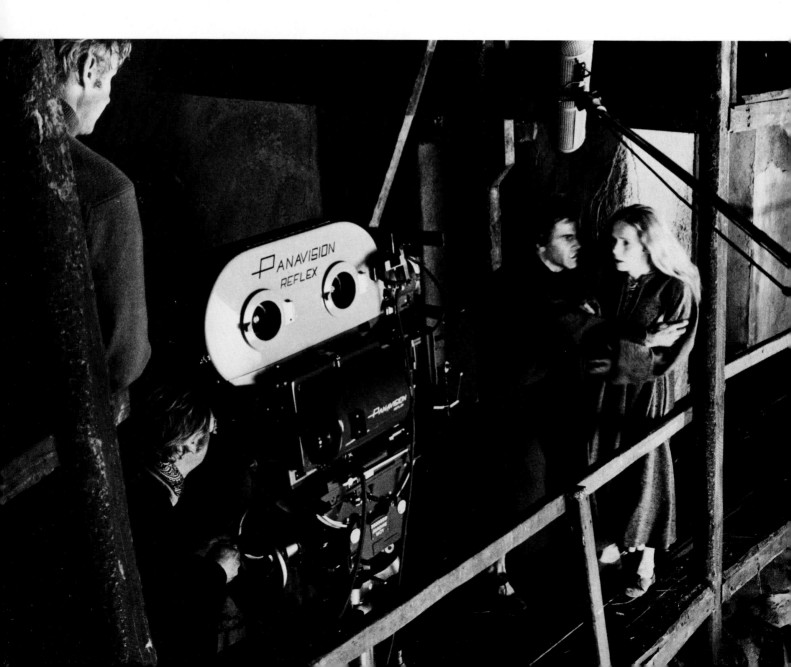

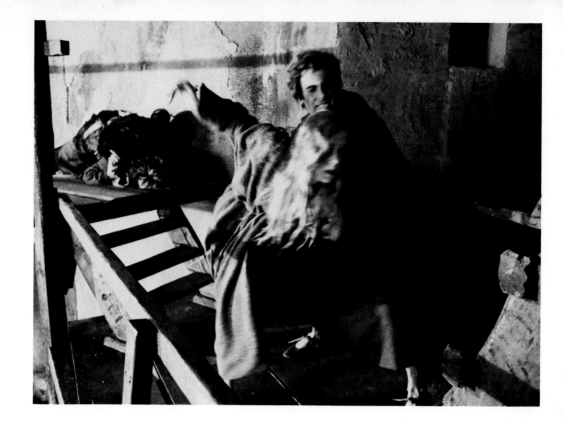

Production: ***Pope Joan***
Character: **Joan**
Director: **Michael Anderson**
U.S. release: **August 1972**

*Pope Joan* was put down by critics as a dreadful costume epic. According to Liv Ullmann, however, the film that was released bore little resemblance to the film that was originally made.

"Someone with no artistic connection with the film ruined it. When it was cut by the director it was a beautiful picture. But someone else took it for six months and recut it, redid the music, and it came out a completely different picture.

"All the modern part of the story was taken out, which took away a lot of the sense of the movie. It was the story of a girl who starts following Christian leaders, then begins preaching herself, has a mental breakdown. In the director's version there is intercutting between the modern girl and her vision. It is the story of a woman in an asylum who *thought* she was Pope Joan. When that was cut away you are left with the story within a story, which makes for a strange story.

"The original film was made with the best care—one of the world's best photographers, wonderful music by Maurice Jarre, a good director. I loved doing it, cared for it, believed in it, and I am very sorry for what happened to it."

Production: **The Emigrants**
Character: **Kristina**
Director: **Jan Troell**
U.S. release: **September 1972**

Production: **The New Land**
Character: **Kristina**
Director: **Jan Troell**
U.S. release: **October 1973**

*The Emigrants* and *The New Land* are presented here together because, although they were released separately, they were filmed simultaneously. The photographs show: Ullmann with Max von Sydow in front of a statue of Kristina and Karl Oscar in Skane; during the first reading of the script; at a lunch break for the cast; with the author Vilhelm Moberg; and after a midwinter press conference. *Time* reviewed the two films a year apart, yet had almost identical reactions to Liv Ullmann's performances. On *The Emigrants*: "... She does not so much master the character of Kristina as she invents her. At the beginning, she is supposed to be still in her teens; without makeup or camera tricks, she conveys the image of youth as she rides casually

on an old swing. The secret is all in the way she grips the ropes with light confidence and catches the rhythm of the swing as if her body had no weight at all. It is a small moment, but in such small moments does Liv demonstrate her virtuosity." On *The New Land:* ". . . Once again there are superb performances, by Axberg, Von Sydow, and by Ullmann, who has one scene trying on a large, fancy hat that could stand as a whole course in the art of acting. At first she is shy and clumsy under the loudly elegant thing, then enchanted, then, for just a moment, a little sad. She makes the viewer understand from just a look that this woman is coming into contact with a whole style of living that is destined to remain forever alien to her."

The scenes from the two films cover the life of Kristina and Karl Oscar until, at the age of forty-five, after bearing nine children, Kristina dies.

With Ingmar Bergman portrait in the background, Liv Ullmann accepts an award of 5000 kroner from the Swedish Film Industry for her portrayal of Kristina in *The Emigrants/The New Land*. Below, in Cannes with Omar Sharif and friend.

Production:   *Cries and Whispers*
Character:   **A sister**
Director:   **Ingmar Bergman**
U.S. release:   **December 1972**

These photographs were taken between filming sequences of *Cries and Whispers*. Two are of actress and director. The one above shows better than any other in this book the details of technique that the actress must be conscious of at the same time she is giving interpretation to the lines. Liv Ullmann has written: "I love technical challenge. Stop on a chalk mark in the middle of a difficult emotional scene. Know all the time where the camera is and in which angle I should be in relation to it.

"Feel inside me a voice directing and at the same time surrender to a situation that has never been mine; although from now on it will be part of my life experience, as if it had happened in reality."

## Portfolio

This is a book of an actress's *oeuvre*. It is only sparsely dotted with photos of moments away from the stage and camera. There are few of the typical family scrapbook pictures. Why? First, because they do not belong here. And second, after perusing the chronicle of production dates one notes that there is very little vacation time in the twenty-two years. As one play runs, another is in rehearsal. Finally, who was to click the shutter during the rare moments of relaxation? Her family, as she has written, is small and often in another place.

The next eight pages contain photographs taken during free time. They are not snapshots. They are intended to provide a montage of Liv Ullmann without, for once, the onus of the part, caught in a moment— aware of the photographer, and so Liv Ullmann aware —frozen in time.

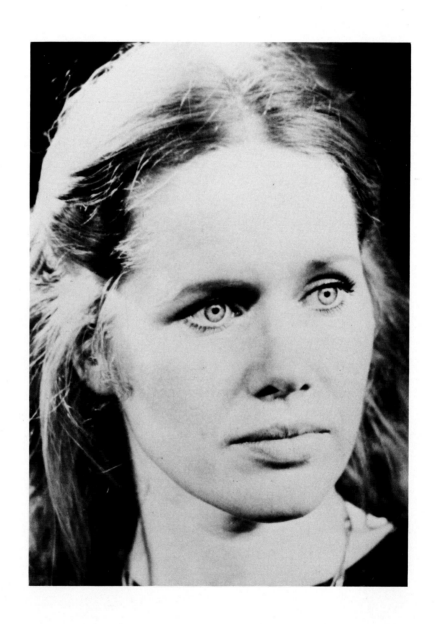

Production: ***Lost Horizon***
Character: **Catherine**
Director: **Charles Jarrott**
U.S. release: **March 1973**

*Lost Horizon*, in this expensive musical remake, lost most of its original charm. It also was a gigantic flop, which may be a good thing for those who felt that it tarnished the novel by James Hilton. The cast, as is usual with Ullmann films successful or otherwise, was superior: in addition to herself, it was led by Peter Finch, Charles Boyer, and John Gielgud.

Any remake always presumes a little arrogance on the part of the producer. In the case at hand this is borne out by his comment about his leading lady: "As soon as I met her, I knew that if she would let me I could make her the most attractive woman on screen. I decided to take a chance on her because I wanted to launch another Ingrid Bergman." This about a woman who had just completed her twenty-ninth play and twenty-fourth film.

Production: **Brand, by Henrik Ibsen**
Character: **Agnes**
Director: **Bjørn Endresson**
Premiere: **Oslo, February 16 and 17, 1973**

*Brand* marked Liv Ullmann's return to Norway from Hollywood. Commentators at the time suggested that the play should have been renamed *Agnes*, such was the publicity attending the homecoming actress. The double premiere was also a result of Liv Ullmann's renown as the Norwegian star who had returned from Hollywood.

Production: **Forty Carats**
Character: **Ann Stanley**
Director: **M. Katselas**
U.S. release: **June 1973**

Production: **A Doll's House, by Henrik Ibsen**
Character: **Nora**
Director: **Pål Skjønberg/Elizabeth Bang**
Premiere: **Oslo, January 24, 1974**

Liv Ullmann has played *A Doll's House* three times: once on radio, this stage production in Oslo, and on Broadway. It is the only play she has repeated and is one with which she has been strongly identified. In its cover story of her, *Time* compared her private life with Nora's, and others have done likewise.

Three of the pictures are from the final act of the play and show some of the range of emotions that buffet Nora as events mount inexorably to lead her to walk out of the door, away from home, husband, and children.

Facing page: Some critics have noted that Ullmann's interpretation of the part tends to weld the acts together by introducing longing amid the early happy scenes. She has said: "In the scene with Kristina, Nora keeps repeating 'I'm so happy.' I doubt very much that Ibsen isn't so clever and so wise about people that if he gives the line 'I'm so happy' over and over you are *not* happy. So I play against it." This picture of Nora, behind the tinsel of the Christmas tree she has just decorated, is full of foreboding.

Right: Returning from a costume ball, Nora is kissed by her husband and the love she feels is mixed with the sad knowledge that their relationship is about to undergo a violent test.

Page 122, top: Moments later her husband confronts her with fury. What she has done out of love for him he ridicules and castigates:

Nora: I've loved you more than anything in the world.
Helmer: Now don't let's have any silly excuses.

In that second, Nora realizes that it has never been a true marriage, that "our home has been nothing but a playroom. I've been your doll-wife here. . . ."

Bottom: The play ends as Nora, having told her husband that for eight years she has been living with a stranger, returns her wedding ring, puts on her coat, and walks out the door.

"I believe that Nora's most beautiful declaration and act of love is leaving her husband.

"She says goodbye to everything that is familiar and secure. She does not walk through the door to find somebody else to live with and for; she is leaving the house more insecure than she ever realized she could be. But she hopes to find out who she is and why she is."

(A Doll's House)

Production: ***Zandy's Bride***
Character: **Hannah Lund**
Director: **Jan Troell**
U.S. release: **May 1974**

Hollywood has a tendency to be formula-bound. It never seems to voyage far in the search for new ideas: Ullmann is being compared to Garbo? Cast her in a remake of *Queen Christina.* (Did Broadway use the same logic to select *Anna Christie* for her?) Jan Troell and Ullmann have created an epic poem in *The Emigrants/The New Land,* ergo get them into town to do another. It was called *Zandy's Bride,* and it failed. Ullmann got good reviews for her role and she likes the film. In part it failed because Jan Troell, who had directed the earlier films, had also photographed them and edited them. Union rules in Hollywood, however, forbade him to touch either the camera or the cutting table.

Union rules could not, however, stop Liv Ullmann from insisting on being her own "stunt woman." Thus, in the scene where Hannah falls from a fast-moving horse and where on foot she heads off a stampede of cattle, it is Ullmann herself that we are watching.

(Zandy's Bride)

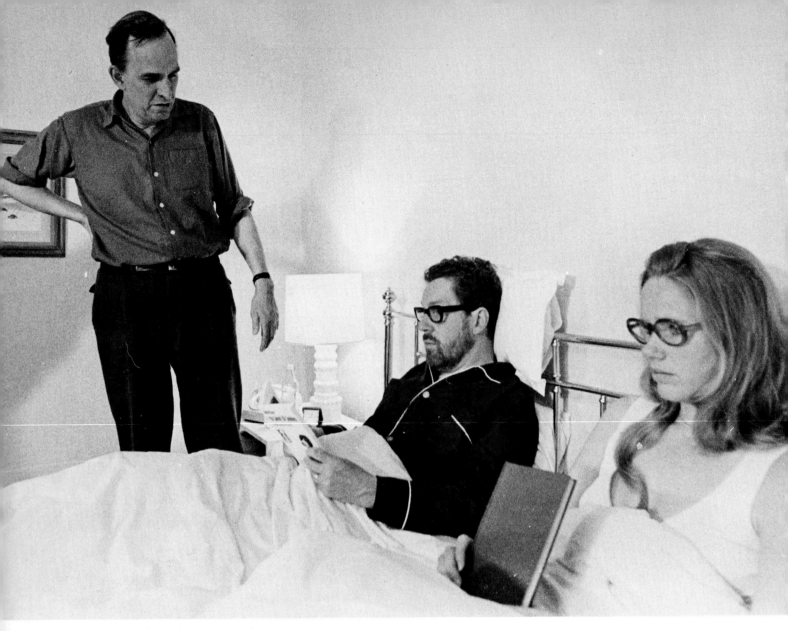

Production: ***Scenes from a Marriage***
Character: **Marianne**
Director: **Ingmar Bergman**
U.S. release: **September 1974**

*Scenes from a Marriage* was, in many ways, Liv Ull-mann's debut to the American audience. It is true that she had featured in five of Ingmar Bergman's earlier films which had appeared in an art house distribution here; and she had been heralded by a 1972 cover story in *Time*. That article was perceptive of her dramatic talent but misjudged the arrival schedule of "Holly-wood's new Nordic star."

*Scenes* brought Ullmann to town. Many people found the film a body blow to the complexity of marriage in their own lives. Many identified with Marianne, the wife in the story; and many critics sought to connect Ull-mann's private life with Bergman to the film's charac-ters. Across America, men and women felt kinship with the woman on the screen.

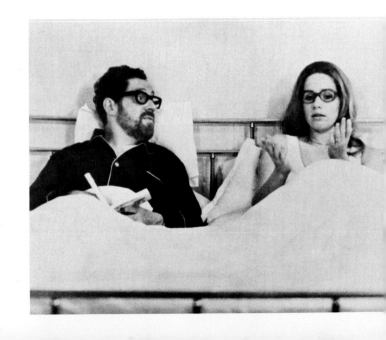

Unfortunately, because of a technicality in the by-laws of the Academy of Motion Picture Arts and Sciences, no one connected with *Scenes* was eligible for consideration of an Oscar. Protesting this, the following letter appeared in a *New York Times* advertisement:

"We the undersigned respectfully request that you make Liv Ullmann eligible for Academy Award consideration. We request that you change the rule which now makes ineligible her performance in *Scenes from a Marriage:* signed: Gena Rowlands, Joanne Woodward, Liza Minnelli, Elizabeth Taylor, Sylvia Sidney, Diahann Carroll, Lauren Bacall, Jane Fonda, Glenda Jackson, Ellen Burstyn, Shirley MacLaine, Jennifer Jones, Ingrid Bergman."

The single substantially disappointing fact about the film is that Liv Ullmann was not available when *Scenes* was dubbed in English, and so her voice, its interpretation and intonation, do not accompany the picture in the English version.

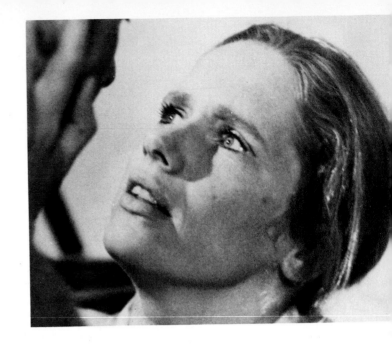

Production: **The Abdication**
Character: **Queen Christina**
Director: **Anthony Harvey**
Premiere: **New York, October 1974**

*The Abdication* is Liv Ullmann's best American film. Subtlety is at work in the development of the character, and Queen Christina's duel/duet with Cardinal Azzolino (Peter Finch) is rich in the counterplay of passion and love. Part of the blame for the film's failure must rest with the timing of its release: just after critics had completed their glowing reviews of *Scenes from a Marriage*. By comparison *The Abdication* was *manqué*, a fact that did not escape the review columns the next day. However, the film must be catalogued as a success in Liv Ullmann's adherence to her credo of acting in the face of the Hollywood idiom. And she herself has emphasized in interviews that it remains one of her favorite films.

The off-camera photos on pages 130-33 show her waiting for the technicians to get ready; pensive moments; having fun in the costume; falling in it on the way to the dressing room; with her daughter.

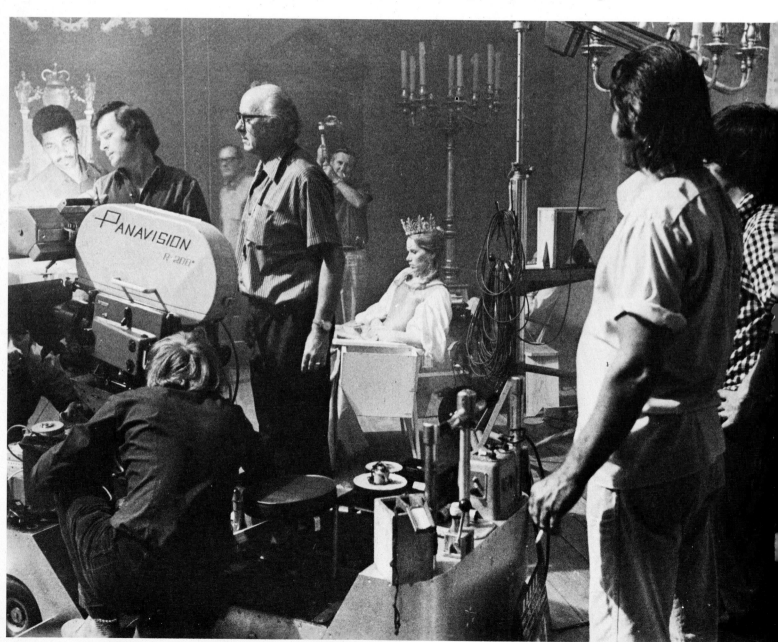

Production: ***A Doll's House***, by Henrik Ibsen
Character: **Nora Helmer**
Director: **Tormod Skagestad**
Premiere: **Philadelphia, January 31, 1975; New York, March 5, 1975**

"I think my Nora in New York was better than in Oslo. Working on the play in a new language helped me because I had to start from a completely new set of references. Also, because the play is not as well known as it is in Norway, where it is part of us, I had to build for that."

The play was sold out for its entire engagement before it opened in New York following a two-week run in Philadelphia, her United States point of debut in theater. The play was well received there at the Zellerbach Theater, but other circumstances were gloomy. The cast was housed in a sleazy motor inn, in which one of them was raped by an intruder. Liv Ullmann's room in daytime was the meeting place for agents, interviewers, critics; but at night looked no different from the resting place of a million traveling salesmen.

In the scenes here, Nora, through flattery, is trying to wheedle some money out of her husband; dancing the tarantella; and returning from the ball in the final act (seconds after the same scene illustrated from the Norwegian production).

In Stavanger with Hubert Humphrey as part of the 150th anniversary celebration of the first Norwegian organized emigration to America; in Hollywood with Charlton Heston, the King of Sweden, and Clint Eastwood.

Production: **_Face to Face_**
Character: **Jenny**
Director: **Ingmar Bergman**
New York premiere: **February 1976**

_Face to Face,_ the story of a woman's mental collapse and slow reconstitution, is probably Liv Ullmann's greatest technical achievement as an actress. The camera is very close on her face and never wavers; and some of the most intense dramatic moments were accomplished in one long take.

"It's very difficult to laugh. It's much easier to cry. Or to have the sound of crying. But you don't think of the technique while you do it; that belongs to your homework. . . . That [referring to the scene] isn't even my laughter. It just came out of my throat that way. But being rid of that technical problem—it took me years to know how to laugh and I still don't always know how to. But having learned it, I don't have to think about it, worry about it. And then when that scene comes I don't have the stress, that 'Oh, I must make this sound like a laugh.' Now the laugh comes like the cry comes. I can live in the scene [and] I'm free to make choices and I can laugh and cry without being stopped by technical limitations. For me, that scene in _Face to Face_ was a great breakthrough."

(Face to Face)

Making a legend; backstage with her mother after a performance; being congratulated by Henry Kissinger at the premiere of *Face to Face;* with Bibi Andersson in Antibes after the Cannes Film Festival off-competition showing of *Face to Face;* in Cannes.

Production: **Pygmalion, by George Bernard Shaw**
Character: **Eliza Doolittle**
Director: **Henning Moritzen**
Premiere: **Stockholm, September 19, 1975**

It was, as *Pygmalion* should be, a happy production. In the Stockholm presentation, the thick cockney tongue of Eliza the flower girl was changed to a heavy Norwegian accent in the Swedish language. Erland Josephson was a bouncy Higgins and it was a pleasant experience to see him in this role after the summitry with Ullmann in *Scenes from a Marriage*.

It was during the daytime hours before the play that Liv Ullmann the author wrote her final draft of *Changing*.

Production: **A Moon for the Misbegotten,**
**by Eugene O'Neill**
Character: **Josie**
Director: **José Quintero**
Premiere: **Oslo, February 10, 1976**

This was the first of four stage collaborations between Liv Ullmann and director José Quintero. She has this to say of her director:

"Of all the people I have ever met, the capacity of love is in him. More than any other director, he is the living proof of it. Ingmar writes something, makes the film about it, coaches you to get things out, listens to you, looks at you, makes you want to give. But he never, never tells about himself to enable you to be brave enough to show yourself. José will dare to go into a half-hour speech about how someone left him, his mouth went dry, he vomited all over the floor. He gives so much of himself to give the actors the courage to give back. He shows himself naked, gives himself away so that you can be brave—make a fool of yourself.

"I loved doing *Moon for the Misbegotten.* I loved the play. The production was not secure enough because we had a short rehearsal time, so it was not the same from night to night. But I liked the part because it had a lot to do with me. It had to do with a 'big elephant,' I thought. Josie isn't really. I wanted to build up the ele-

phant thing, and José said no, no, no: *she* thinks she is an elephant. It is inside her, not outside.

"That is why Josie is beautiful once, when her love is asleep in her arms. Then she is no more the elephant, she is a madonna. We are what we think we are. You don't see the elephant in me because I am successful, you don't see it if you don't know me well. It is why it was so wonderful to do her and have that moment—which is almost my favorite moment in theater—where she has him on the stairs in her lap."

Wrote one critic of this performance: "Miss Ullmann is of slender figure and gentle features, but such is her art that she evokes the image of the dominating giantess of clumsy gait, awkward gestures, a lunatic glint in her far-away glance. It is an amazingly complete interpretation, realizing all the diverse facets of the part: its robust humor, its wistful yearning, its physical strength and its maternal tenderness. It is a performance of profound theatrical understanding, drawing on deep emotional wells."

Production: **A Bridge Too Far**
Character: **Kate ter Horst**
Director: **Richard Attenborough**
New York premiere: **June 1977**

*A Bridge Too Far* featured a lengthy roster of excellent actors cast in cameo roles. Liv Ullmann played the Dutch World War II heroine Kate ter Horst. The real-life Kate ter Horst came to the location and is pictured with Liv Ullmann. She is also seen here in moments from the film with Laurence Olivier, who played Dr. Spaander.

Production: **Anna Christie, by Eugene O'Neill**
Character: **Anna Christie**
Director: **José Quintero**
New York premiere: **April 17, 1977**

The first photograph is of the cast, in costume, with director José Quintero. The others, from the production, come to life after reading the interview.

(Anna Christie)

Offstage moments: with Lynn Redgrave after the opening of her play *Knock, Knock*; with President Carter after a performance of *Anna Christie*; as honorary marshal on Norway Day in Brooklyn; upon publication of her book, *Changing*.

Production: **The Serpent's Egg**
Character: **Manuela Rosenberg**
Director: **Ingmar Bergman**
New York premiere: **January 1978**

Production: **_Rosmersholm_, by Henrik Ibsen**
Character: **Rebekka**
Director: **Bjørn Endresson**
Premiere: **Trondhjem, February 3, 1978**

_Rosmersholm_ is one of Ibsen's most complex and difficult plays. Rebekka West's suicide in the final act is not obviously foreshadowed in the script. Thus the actors must carefully prepare for it in the earlier scenes or it makes no sense. Freud wrote extensively about Rebekka. Shaw considered _Rosmersholm_ Ibsen's best play.

This production was very stark: as the photographs show, the stage was barren of furniture, paintings, the tangible evidences of Rosmer's home, where the action takes place. The actors were placed in statuary positions on the stage in some kind of Scando-Grecian style.

"I was unhappy with the production because it was stylized and I hate a style that restricts the actor. Our tools were taken away from us. I would love to play Brecht in a stylized form. But with Brecht and a real Brecht director you would have a reason for doing what is stylized. Style can be wonderful to be part of, but to me this _Rosmersholm_ was a series of restricted actions. I would love to play Rebekka again. It is one of the greatest stories of love. Rebekka is destructive in her love—I mean, she makes another woman go and commit suicide by telling lies to her—but she is a woman whose passion comes from the deepest core."

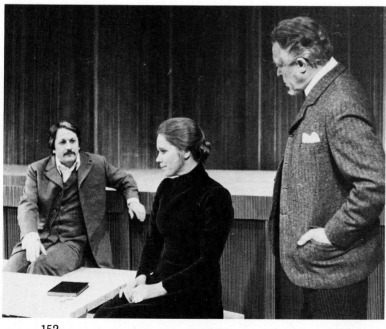

Production: **Autumn Sonata**
Character: **Eva**
Director: **Ingmar Bergman**
New York premiere: **October 1978**

Ingmar Bergman collaborates with his two actresses, in a searing examination of the relationship between a mother (Ingrid Bergman) and daughter.

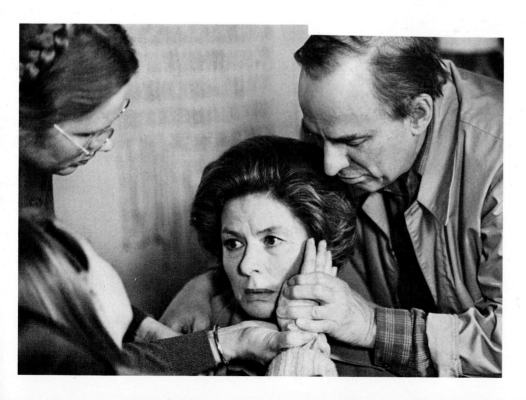

153

She has an apartment in Oslo, but is not often there. Usually she is living in New York, Munich, Stockholm, or some other work location. Even when she can be in Oslo, home continues to be a small house high on a cliff overlooking the ocean that spills into the long bay of Sandefjord.

Production: ***Lady from the Sea,*** **by Henrik Ibsen**
Character: **Elida Wangel**
Director: **Per Bronken**
              **In production**

Production: ***The Bear,*** **by Anton Chekhov**
Character: **Elena Popova**
Director: **José Quintero**
Premiere: **Melbourne, November 1, 1978**

*The Bear* is a one-act farce: an oats merchant arrives at a widow's house to collect a past-due bill. They fall in love; the end. The entertainment is carried by the counterplay between the hulking man—the Bear—and the widow, who with dramatic resolution has encased herself in black. In this production Madame Popova fairly shone in the martyrdom of her mourning. It is a rare example of Liv Ullmann using makeup: "I use it on purpose. The widow loves mourning, she knows it suits her very well. So she makes herself pale and with big open eyes. But it isn't Liv using makeup to create the character; it is the character herself using makeup. The Bear even remarks, 'You haven't forgotten to powder your nose.'"

Liv Ullmann played the comedy well and with the subtlety of her heavier roles. In one marvelous but fleeting moment, for example, when the butler tells her they are falling to pieces by remaining behind black curtains, Madame Popova takes her teaspoon and, ever so quickly, checks her appearance in its reflection.

Production: ***The Human Voice,* by Jean Cocteau**
Character: **A woman**
Director: **José Quintero**
Premiere: **Melbourne, November 1, 1978**
**New York, January 14, 1979**

*The Human Voice* premiered in Melbourne on November 1, 1978, and ended its run in Sydney on December 16. As Liv Ullmann's most recent work it is the proper end to this book, but it is also an appropriate summation of her career to date. The play is a monodrama of a woman on the telephone with the man she loves, who has left her. Such is the power of the performance that we not only die inwardly with the woman, but we know the man. In this forty-five-minute soliloquy, from the opening ring of the phone the audience is caught in one long relationship with the face of this woman as it ranges from an early radiant sweetness to a final broken sobbing hysteria. Part of the power of Liv Ullmann's creation of the character is the dignity the woman brings to the totality of love that she unfolds into the telephone.

"She fights, but she doesn't fight in a way other women would, asking for pity, asking for bad conscience from him. It is unlike how most men and women would react, how I would react. Early in the rehearsals after the line where she says she has taken pills, but don't worry, I'm fine, I kept forgetting to say 'Oh my poor darling who I've hurt so much.' I forgot lines like that because subconsciously *I* thought it was too much. But I think it is a true story of an ordinary little woman who becomes great because she knows how to love the way Erich Fromm talks about love: that love is giving, not expecting. And when the play ends her blood, so to speak, is all over the stage. She is bleeding alone and trying as best she can not to have him bleed or to see her bleeding."

The play ends. The ripped, lost woman of love has collapsed on her bed. The curtain falls on *The Human Voice*. Applause. Curtain calls. The house lights rise, the audience moves toward the exits. Liv Ullmann goes to her dressing room. She changes from the nightgown of the play into street clothes. Then, sitting before the mirror, she puts on a little makeup.

# Photo Credits

The photos herein are courtesy of the following sources.
In the cases where a number of photos come from a single source
they are identified by this legend:

A —Unidentified or private
B —M. A. Høiland
C —Sturlason
D —Sturlason, courtesy of the Norwegian Theater
E —Jan Schwarzott, courtesy of the National Theater
F —A.S Norsk Telegrambyrå
G —Otto Carlmar
H —UPI
I —Cinematograph A.B. Fårö
J —Pressens Bild, Stockholm
K —Warner Bros., Inc., copyright © 1972
L —Svensk Pressfoto
M —Columbia Pictures Industries, Inc.
N —Dino de Laurentiis Corporation
O —Martha Swope
P —Warner Bros., Inc., copyright © 1973
Q —Warner Bros., Inc., copyright © 1975

Pages 2-3: Tor Gulliksrud. 37-38: A. 40: 1 A, 2 B. 41: 1-3 G. 42: 1-2 B. 43: 1-2 B. 44: 1-4 B. 45: 1 B, 2 Willy Myrron. 46: 1 F, 2-3 B. 47: A. 48: 1-3 G. 49: G. 50: 1-2 B. 51: A. 52: 1-2 B. 53: 1 C, 2 D. 54: 1 A, 2 F, 3 G. 55: 1-2 Ess-Film A/S. 56: C. 57: 1-2 D. 58: 1-2 © Sandrew Film & Teater AB. 59: 1-2 D. 60: D. 61: C. 62: 1-2 D, 3 C, 4 D. 63: 1-2 D. 64: D. 65: C. 66: 1-2 D. 67: 1-3 D. 68: E. 69: 1-2 E. 70: E. 71: E. 72: 1-2 E. 73: E. 74: 1-3 Norsk Rikskringkasting. 75: 1-5 Norsk Rikskringkasting. 76: 1-2 A. 77: 1 F, 2 H. 78: I. 79: 1-2 I. 80: 1-2 I. 81: A. 82: 1-2 A, 4-5 Åke Hylén, 3 Bo Vibenius. 83: Bo Vibenius. 84: Åke Hylén. 85: Åke Hylén. 86: 1-2 I. 87: 1 A, 2-3 E. 88: 1-2 E. 89: 1-2 E. 90: E. 91: 1 J, 2 A. 92: 1-2 A. 93: 1-2 I. 94: 1-2 I. 95: 1-2 I. 96: 1 Emerson Film Enterprises, Inc., 2 H, 3 A. 97: 1-3 E. 98: 1 M, 2 A. 99: 1-2 A. 100: 1-3 A, 4 Ove Wallin. 101: 1 K, 2 J, 3 K. 102: 1-2 K, 3 AB Svensk Filmindustri. 103: 1-3 K. 104: 1 J, 2 Pierre Manciet.

105: 1-2 I. 106: 1-2 L. 107: L. 108: 1 Istvan Breznitz, 2 Margret Tenbub. 109: A. 110: A. 111: Victor Skrebneski. 112: *Paris-Match*. 113: Leonard de Raemy/SYGMA. 114: Eva Sereny/SYGMA. 115: Bob Burchette of *The Washington Post*. 116: A. 117: 1-3 M. 118: C. 119: M. 120: D. 121: D. 122: 1-2 C. 123: Q. 124: 1-2 Q. 125: 1-3 Q, 4 Bob Willoughby. 126: 1 J, 2 I. 127: 1-2 I. 128: 1 I, 2 J. 129: 1 P, 2 Eva Sereny/SYGMA. 130: 1-2 P. 131: A. 132: Eva Sereny/SYGMA. 133: 1-3 J, 4 P. 134: 1-3 The Joseph Abeles Collection. 135: 1 F, 2 J. 136: I. 137: I. 138: 1-2 I. 139: I. 140: 1 Bill King, 2 Stig Naess, VG, Norway, 3 A, 4 H. 141: Philippe Ledru/SYGMA. 142: 1-3 J. 143: 1-2 C. 144: 1-2 Joseph E. Levine Presents, Inc., 3-4 Adrie H. Nab. 145: 1-2 O. 146: O. 147: 1-2 O. 148: 1 A, 2 H. 149: 1 H, 2 *Paris-Match*, 3 A. 150: 1-3 N. 151: N. 152: 1-3 Roar Ohlander. 153: 1-3 Arne Carlsson. 154: 1 Tor Gulliksrud, 2 *Paris-Match*. 155: 1-2 Arne Borsheim. 156: A. 157: Paul Crowley. 158: A.

Grateful acknowledgment for the photographs which appear on the jacket: from *Scenes from a Marriage* to Lars Karlsson, and from *Face to Face* to Arne Carlsson.